THE 4TH

The 4th Level of Financial Freedom *is a life changing phenomenon! It will change your outlook on stewardship and on how you manage God's money.* –

Dr. Niares Hunn, Sr. Instructional Designer, St. Charles, Missouri

This book is powerful. The stories are uplifting. A hunger for financial freedom will be created in the hearts and minds of all who read it. –

Sherry A. Jones, Independent Beauty Consultant, Mary Kay, Inc.

What an awesome book. The aspiration I once had to become debt-free has been rekindled. I'm thankful to Adrian and Quaneshala for reawaking my faith. –

Tameka Flemming, Founder, Girls of Virtue Inc.

All I can say is, simply remarkable. The material in this book has revolutionized our church. Adrian and Quaneshala will continue helping others because lives are being transformed, including mine. –

Evangelist Mary Frances Terry, MS & Western Tennessee District Council, Pentecostal Assemblies of the World

No superlative could adequately describe the inspiration this book evokes. The authors write with a rare combination of insight, credibility, wit, and the unpretentious pragmatism of one who has lived it. The book challenges the reader to look beyond instant gratification to a lifestyle that places greater value on making financial decisions for greater prosperity. Certainly a must read for all who aspire to live debt-free! –

Kofi and Christina Boateng,
Silicon Valley Professionals

I was stressed out because I was unable to pay my bills. I was constantly using my credit cards to help make ends meet. It seemed as if I could never get ahead because all of my money was going towards paying off the interest on my bills instead of paying off the principal. Although I had an enormous amount of debt, this book was able to give me hope. Even my situation can be turned around once I apply these simple principles in my life. I'm grateful for the knowledge on how to become a better steward of my finances. –

Sabrena Tucker, Lead Bank Teller,
Tampa, Florida

This book should be read by every married couple. It provides proven biblical principles that will help couples accomplish their financial goals. You will be blessed. –

Jeffery L. Smith, Assistant Pastor,
Christ Temple

I find myself amazed and strangely addicted to reading the stories that mirror my own. This book gave me a deeper understanding of what is seen within most of us today. It is truly an entertaining and informative read that I can pass on to others who need that wake-up call. –

Glendora P. Porter, Supervisor,
Disaster Assistance Loan Officer

I have known this couple for many years. Their work is superb. I am confident that your financial future will be a lot brighter after reading this book. They have the wisdom and experience to bring you into a financial safe haven. –

Jerry Linhares, Pastor,
New Covenant Church

I have learned a plethora of knowledge from this dynamic couple. They lit a fire when they taught a financial workshop at my church. The information was exactly what the doctor ordered. I would recommend this book to anyone that is serious about living a debt-free life. If you are having financial difficulties and your pay check is shorter than it ought to be, they will teach you countermeasure to lengthen it. –

Suffragan Bishop Melvin H. Terry,
Apostolic Assembly of Jesus Christ

If you want to stay on top financially, it would be wise to listen to this couple. They have personally proven that what they are teaching actually works. If it works for them, it can work for the rest of us. My main regret is that they weren't around when I needed them the most. Therefore, I had to make discoveries that cost me time, money, and sweat which resulted in a lot of disappointments. Following their plan will help you make better choices and will enable you to enjoy the fruits of your labor much more. –

Bishop Clifton Jones, Diocesan
of the 10th Episcopal District,
Pentecostal Assemblies of the World

I could not put this book down! It is absolutely outstanding and life changing. It will give you hope and fill you with excitement to start living a debt-free lifestyle immediately! –

Rosalind Ominde, Administrative
Assistant, Department of Aging and
Disability Services

This book is uplifting and encouraging. I was inspired by the technique in which the writers explained financial freedom from a spiritual perspective. –

Lijwana Washington,
Programmer Analyst Advanced,
Orlando, Florida

Most people go through life with a desire to be financially free but have no plan in place to get there. The current state of our economy has brought home the fact that you must increase your knowledge and control your financial destiny. The 4th Level of Financial-Freedom *is an excellent starting point. It is a realistic approach to help you take that very important first step. –*

Cookie Chandler Belle, Partner,
Belle Capital Resources, LLC

I'm thankful to Adrian and Quaneshala for their words of wisdom. I can now see the light at the end of the tunnel. I can't even begin to express how I have been set free. I hope this couple continues to do what they are doing; they are helping so many people. Thank God for His helpers! –

Denise Jones, Teacher,
Dallas Independent School District

God gave Adrian and Quaneshala the wisdom to pay it forward. They continue to do so every day by living the example they put forth in the book. The book provides very insightful techniques on how we can change our financial habits - not have our habits change us. It is an excellent read. –

Shelene A. Thompson,
IT Developer, Atlanta, Georgia

If there is ever a book that can help you alleviate debt and live a debt-free life, it is The 4th Level of Financial Freedom. *I am confident you will find this book insightful and easy to understand. –*

Orlando & Christa Blackburn,
Owners, OB on Air

Look inside to see what Adrian and Quaneshala has given up so that others may see a better way. This book is definitely a must read to a better future. –

Dr. Shirley Durham, Author,
Pastoring from Scratch

I know Adrian and Quaneshala Johnson to be two people of spiritual integrity. Instead of hoarding the God-given financial strategies outlined in this book, they decided to share these principles with the world so that the rest of us can obtain and enjoy financial freedom which results in abundant living. –

Barbara Ann Fields, Author,
40 Reasons How and Why Men and Boys Should Avoid Incarceration

This is the first time in over ten years of being married that we have been able to communicate with each other about our finances. We finally have the blueprint on how to work together as a couple on becoming debt-free and on building wealth. –

Chris & April Gainer, Owners,
Independent Insurance Representative

Being around Adrian and Quaneshala encourages a desire to be debt-free! Make the necessary changes and no matter how hot the fire (test of endurance) gets, stick with it. –

Willie Ruth Wilson, Retired Certified Texas Procurement Manager, Health and Human Services Commission

This book is exactly what is needed in this day and age. Adrian and Quaneshala is a couple with vision and purpose. –

Dr. H. Durham, Pastor, Better Way Apostolic Church

While reading The 4th Level of Financial Feedom, *the tears began to flow. This book contains the truth I needed at a critical time in my life. I pray that its message will have a profound effect on others as well. Although I am a work in progress, I have more hope now than I had before reading this book. I commit to no longer living in survival mode from day to day. My new ambition is to successfully conquer my financial problems for myself and for my children. I am in the right place for change to happen; I can almost taste sweet victory around the corner. God Bless the labor of your hands. –*

Merline Antenor, IT Project
Management Professional,
Austin, Texas

Adrian & Quaneshala have a gift for making the complexity of managing your finances seem extremely simple. Their simplistic teaching makes transforming your financial future easy and fun. This book will certainly persuade individuals to make the tough, but necessary, changes that lead to financial freedom. –

Billy G. Newton, Diocesan of the
29th Episcopal District,
Pentecostal Assemblies of the World

THE 4TH LEVEL OF FINANCIAL FREEDOM

SECRETS FROM THE HEART OF A TEACHER

THE 4TH LEVEL OF FINANCIAL FREEDOM

ADRIAN & QUANESHALA JOHNSON

FOREWORD BY MICHELLE PRINCE

Nairda Publishing
Arlington, TX

ISBN: 978-0-615-42330-2

www.The4thLevelOfFinancialFreedom.com

LEGAL DISCLAIMER

Am I willing to give up what I have in order to be what I am not yet? Am I able to follow the spirit of love into the desert? It is a frightening and sacred moment. There is no return. One's life is charged forever. It is the fire that gives us our shape.

– Mary Richards

ACKNOWLEDGMENTS

We would like to thank everyone who assisted in the creation of this book. We really appreciate all the advice, encouragement, kind words, stories, testimonies, and prayers. Most of all, we would like to thank God for giving us the insight of understanding how to build wealth and a passion for helping others create financial freedom in their own lives.

CONTENTS

FOREWORD

This could be the day that changes your Financial Destiny forever. How can I make such a bold statement, you may ask? It's simply because you have begun to read *The 4th Level of Financial Freedom* by Adrian and Quaneshala Johnson. *The 4th Level of Financial Freedom* was written to help individuals transform their relationship with money forever. Adopting the philosophies in this book will teach you how to handle money with wisdom.

Most people believe that it takes an enormous amount of money in order to live financially free. That's simply not true. Living financially free has little to do with the income you make, but everything to do with the belief system you currently hold about money. I'm sure you have heard the saying "If you divided up all of the money in the world equally among everyone, it would soon end up back into the same hands." What a true and profound statement. Think of it this way. The capacity to generate and maintain wealth will seldom surpass one's own development. If you don't believe me, observe the people who have won millions playing the lottery. They are almost always destined to lose all of their winnings unless they quickly develop a millionaire mindset. Otherwise, the inevitable is bound to happen.

Adrian and Quaneshala have both the knowledge and the personal experiences to help you transform your financial situation. They not only believe, but live by the same sound and practical principles they teach. They have been completely debt-free, including their house, for years. Their debt-free lifestyle has not only changed their lives, but has also revolutionized the lives of everyone they have come in contact with. It does not take being around them long before you begin to sense their genuine sincerity for improving the financial well-being of others.

If you are ready to take the next step toward the lifestyle of financial freedom that you deserve, read this book in its entirety. Apply the secrets hidden inside. You now hold within your hands the very tools that can help you create the life of your dreams. Opportunity is knocking at the door. The question is, "Will you be bold enough to answer?"

Michelle Prince, Best-Selling Author,
Winning In Life Now,
Professional Speaker & Mentor,
www.WinningInLifeNow.com

A WORD FROM THE AUTHORS

Let me start off by saying how honored we are that you are taking the time to read this life changing book. The mere fact that you picked it up reveals to us that you are someone who is interested in being a student of the wealth building process. Reading this book will put you way ahead of the curve. Most people would rather spend more time planning a vacation than planning their financial destiny. So, congratulations for being one step ahead of the crowd.

Inside the pages of this book, you will learn the secrets that we have discovered over the years by our intense study of wealth accumulation. Before beginning this journey, take heed of this warning: this is not a "get-rich-quick" scheme. This book is designed to help you slowly and steadily build your financial future over time. It all begins with you making the right financial decisions. Notice that we use the word "build." That's right. You will have to work at it day in and day out in order to have long-term success. Our focus is to help you change your old destructive money habits and teach you how to develop new constructive ones.

While reading this book, please do not skip over sections that you feel do not apply to you. Reading each page carefully will ensure that you will not miss any of the concepts that are outlined in each succeeding chapter. Plus, you never know which sentence will lead to an idea that will hold the key to your breakthrough.

Some of the material contained in this book has been written strictly from my perspective and point of view. A number of events that are included in this book happened before Quaneshala and I were married. For instance, you will notice that throughout this book we use words such as "I" and "my" when it relates to experiences we had while single. The sections where we use the words "we" or "our" refer to events after we were married. We also collaborated together in the sections of this book where Quaneshala and I are mentioned together.

Quaneshala played a very influential part in helping with the creation of this book. She brought in a lot of witty ideas that I'm certain I never would have thought of in a million years. Without her, I seriously doubt that I could have single handedly crafted such a beautiful manuscript that we are both exceptionally proud of. It has been a true pleasure having my wife, friend, and life companion to partner with me in writing this book.

We do hope that you will enjoy reading and applying these financial principles to your own life. We certainly enjoyed sharing them. Our sincere desire is that the contents of this book will plant a seed in each reader to not only pursue wealth, but to also obtain financial abundance. This is now your personal "go-to" book for financial wisdom. Please take full advantage of it by reading it many times over. If you are ready to start on the journey to financial independence, we are confident that the contents of this book will help you achieve remarkable results.

INTRODUCTION

One Sunday morning while at church, the Pastor told everyone to imagine what it would feel like if God paid off their biggest debt. Quaneshala looked at me, shrugged her shoulders, and said, "Oh, the light bill." I wish you could have seen the expression on her face. It was like the spirit of freedom was overshadowing her. How amazing is that? We only have to worry about earning enough money to pay our utility bills. That's a kind of freedom I cannot describe.

This was a special moment for me because we had just paid off our house a few weeks prior. We did it after being married for only two years. It's amazing how our friends thought we were crazy when they learned of our simplistic lifestyle. They once considered us to be extremely frugal, even "cheap." Now they are amazed at our accomplishments. The best part about it is that the victory came a month before my thirty-second birthday. We went on vacation and celebrated for two weeks. The sacrifices we made in order to pay off our home were well worth it.

People constantly ask me what it feels like to have my home paid in full. I simply say, "It's like living a dream." We have been able to do so many amazing things since becoming debt-free. I am astonished when I think about the decisions I postponed because of my bondage to debt. I literally held myself back from making life-changing decisions such as pursuing my dream of becoming a Financial Life Coach, author, and speaker. Now, however, living debt-free has released a freedom inside of me that words cannot describe.

I believe that this way of life is for everyone. If you would have asked me five years ago whether I thought this style of life was possible, I would have answered in the negative. That negative view has been changed. I know that anything is possible to those who believe. The fact that I obtained financial freedom is the main reason we launched our company, Financial Counseling from The Heart of a Teacher. Our mission is to give others HOPE in a better future and the COURAGE to make that future a reality.

If you are ready to get rid of the shackles that bind you and keep you debt ridden, keep reading this book with a prepared heart, an open mind, and with an excited spirit. Our plan is a tried and proven one. You, too, can step into a life of abundance and blessings. If you accepted this challenge and work this plan, please write and let us know about your journey. We'd love to know how this book has impacted your life. Your testimonials fuel the fire that burns inside of our hearts. It's a fire that desires to see everyone delivered from financial bondage. You are the reason we give our all to this ministry.

LEVEL 1:
THE TRANSFORMATION BEGINS

ADRIAN'S STORY

As a teenager, I thought that financial problems were a normal part of life. It seemed as if everyone around me had debt. I grew up with the impression that, as an adult, I should spend all the money I could get my hands on. Temporary gratification that came from buying stuff was all I had to look forward to. Somewhere along the line, I missed the important principle of saving money, and not just for the proverbial rainy day.

When I finally became independent and started paying my own bills, I began to practice all of the bad habits that I had learned from watching others manage their money. I had several maxed out credit cards, a motorcycle debt, student loan debt, and a mortgage hanging over my head. After accumulating all of this debt, it wasn't long before I became aware of the negative effect debt can have on a person's life. I had to face a harsh reality: I was not making wise decisions with money.

In 2005, I finally had enough of living from paycheck to paycheck. At that time, I was over $125,000 in debt (including the mortgage). I was now sick and tired of living in this condition of constantly juggling bill payments. I was giving myself immediate pleasure by spending money that was not mine. I was a slave to my creditors and I decided that enough was enough. I had to face the facts. I was working for everyone but Adrian. I was the only one who was not keeping any money. In other words, I was getting poorer while all of my creditors were getting richer. I was tired of being broke. During my lowest moment, I made the decision

I was over $125,000 in debt

to turn my life around forever. I decided that once I became debt-free, I would remain debt-free. I would never put myself in that scary and dangerous financial position again.

After less than two years of sacrifice, I am proud to say that I paid off over $35,000 of debt. That's not including the $4,000 I used to cash flow our wedding expenses. So, here I was, debt-free (all except the house), with a new beautiful bride. That was an awesome feeling.

But that's not the end of the story. Three weeks after our two-year anniversary, we were able to become totally debt-free. That's right! We paid off the remaining balance of $90,000 on our mortgage in two years. After reaching this goal, I was finally convinced that the only limits to obtaining financial freedom we have are the limits we place on ourselves.

QUANESHALA'S STORY

Growing up, I always had a desire to help others travel down the road that leads to financial freedom. Throughout my life, I saw countless people making the same financial mistakes over and over again. The Bible states, "People perish for the lack of knowledge." *If people only knew that there is a better way to live with money*, I thought. *With the right financial knowledge, people could enjoy a debt-free lifestyle.*

I can remember advising individuals about their finances as early as junior high school. I was well received by many of my peers because they knew I practiced what I preached. By applying the principles of God, I was able to graduate from college with a B.S. in Computer Information Systems from Florida Agricultural and Mechanical University, and a MBA from Amberton University without acquiring debt.

Financial freedom is for anyone who is willing to sacrifice short term pleasure...

For the rest of my life, I plan on continuing to be a strong advocate for living debt-free. My motto is, "Financial freedom is for anyone who is willing to sacrifice short-term pleasure in order to achieve long-term success." This is the perfect opportunity for me to share my enthusiasm regarding money management in order to help others restore their hope in a brighter tomorrow. Especially in today's economy with so many people losing their jobs, their homes, and their faith, achieving a debt-free life is now more important than ever.

> ***By taking it one day at a time, soon you will end up at the thought first created in your mind.*** **—**
> Adrian Johnson

THE FACTS

I trust that you are now filled with hope and excitement after reading our story. Please realize that I am no different than anyone else, and that you too, can enjoy the same level of success as I have. The truth is, all you have to do is make the same decision I made 10 years ago, namely to take back control of my future. No one can make the decision for you to live financially free. You must decide. Take the advice of Dale Carnegie, one of the wealthiest men in the world who said, "Those convinced against their will are of the same opinion still." In simpler terms, if I make the decision for you, you will remain at the same place you are now.

But the good news is everyone who has achieved financial success had to first make the decision to be a financial success. You're not alone. Many others were once servants to debt, but are now rid of this barrier to living the life they desire. The difference is they had the courage to muster up enough faith, hope, and determination to be freed from bondage. Their stories of triumph live on.

...everyone who has achieved financial success had to first make the decision to be a financial success.

Throughout this book, I have included the success stories of other people. I am sure you will find them encouraging, thought provoking, and enlightening. The story I am most interested in, however, is yours. Imagine yourself as a flower on the verge of blooming. You are a bud just waiting to burst forth and experience the world. That's the reality of your life once you decide to take that first step to financial freedom.

Don't worry about how things are going to work out. Just take the first step. I believe that once you apply the secrets inside this book to your life, you too, will be like the people who came before you. Come on! Step up and add your name to the list of financial achievers. I did it, and so can you!

DESIRE WILL LEAD

At the time of the writing of this particular section of the book, my brother, Ira, had just graduated from high school and was getting ready to go off to college. I wanted him to attend my alma mater, Mississippi State University, in Starkville, Mississippi. I thought this would be the perfect school for him since he was majoring in engineering. I assisted him with all of his paperwork so he would be ready to attend school for the fall semester.

Should he choose to go after what he was passionate about...

During the summer, however, the head coach from another college in Mississippi offered my brother a scholarship to play tennis at his college. Ira was very excited about the offer as tennis is his favorite sport, yet he had a decision to make. Should he choose to go after what he was passionate about, or should he follow in the footsteps of his big brother? After spending a weekend contemplating his options, my brother decided to accept the tennis scholarship.

Initially, I was a little upset about his decision. Personally, I wanted him to focus solely on academics. Nevertheless, after looking at the big picture, I realized I was attempting to make a life decision for him without considering what Ira desired. He really wanted to play college tennis, as this would give him a chance to live out his dream. He assured me that he could still focus on academics because the college he chose also has an engineering department.

MAKE A DECISION

I started this section with the story about my brother because it is a powerful example about someone who was faced with a life-changing decision. Although it has little to do with finances, it has everything to do with the decision making process and having the proper attitude when it comes to making important choices.

Your first step to financial freedom is to decide to be financially free.

Your first step to financial freedom is to decide to be financially free. Now, I am sure you have heard this time and time again about the importance of making a decision. Whether they are big or small, we go through life making decisions every day from sun-up to sundown. Don't take this step lightly. The ability to make an informed choice is the first and most important step you must take in your journey toward financial freedom. Moving forward is impossible until you determine you no longer want to live under your current circumstances.

There is a major difference between someone who is absolutely fed up versus someone who is just playing around with no real or sincere desire to change. You too, most likely have known a person who is committed and takes action, while another non-committed person continues to tell themselves that they will start tomorrow. But tomorrow never comes.

> ***Successful people are successful because they form the habits of doing those things that failures don't like to do. —***
>
> Albert Gray

NEW ACTIONS BRINGS NEW RESULTS

I am sure you have experienced a time in your life when you were hurt by someone. You probably said to yourself, *Never again will I let that person take advantage of me*. Did you make up your mind that you were not going down that road again? You were strengthened by that experience which made you develop an attitude of certainty. No matter what the future held, you were never going to go through that situation again.

On the other hand, has there ever been a moment in your life when you made a halfhearted decision? You may have sincerely wanted to change, but you did not commit 100% to the process. When times got tough, you turned back to that bad habit because it was easier. You see, we all feel safe with all things familiar.

...we all feel safe with all things familiar.

Out of these two examples, what stood out for you? Do you see how changes were easier to make when pain was mixed into the equation? Decide today that your current situation is painful enough for change. Believe it or not, change can happen in a second, leading you to future success. Things may take a little time to manifest, but good results will soon follow your new actions.

Questions to Ponder:

- ❑ Do you want to be completely free from debt?
- ❑ Are you willing to not let others dictate your financial situation?
- ❑ Do you want to be able to retire with dignity?
- ❑ Do you want to leave a financial legacy for your children?

If you can answer yes to the above questions, it's an indication that you have finally had enough of your current situation and are now ready to move forward. True victory follows when a person determines that they have taken all they can take.

Once you have made a decision to be free of financial bondage, the hardest step is over. People only struggle when they have not totally committed to change. Sure, while you are learning these new financial concepts, you are going to face some challenges, but if you are committed to the process, nothing can stop you.

True victory follows when a person determines that they have taken all they can take.

Whatever comes your way you will not back down, quit, or surrender. You are confident that no matter what happens, you are determined to win. That is the exact same approach you will need to succeed in your financial situation. When you begin to adopt the principles taught in this book, it may seem like you are being attacked on every side. It's almost as if life is testing you to see if you are serious about making a change. Will you give up at the first sign of trouble? Will you give in at the moment you have to stand up and defend this new lifestyle you have embraced? Or will you fold under the pressure of family and friends well intentioned but often misplaced advice? Maybe you will be counted among the few that will keep the faith even when it seems as if the odds are not in your favor.

Now that you are at a crossroads, know that you can, and will, move on with the sweet taste of victory in your mouth. There are so many others who have already blazed the path for you. There is nothing new under the sun about obtaining financial freedom. Others have walked down this road even before you made the decision to do the same. Use their stories for encouragement. You can save yourself a lot of heartache and frustration by following their examples.

This journey is all about learning as you go. Of course you may make some mistakes; just don't give up. Endurance is your key to success. Don't let discouragement set in by trying to figure everything out at once. The important thing is to keep moving. If you mess up in one area, start again and again and again until you master each concept.

This journey is all about learning as you go.

This book is not a means to an end; it is merely a starting point. I have laid the foundation for you to build upon. These are the same principles I live by daily, and I have been where you are right now. Yet, I am here to testify that there is a better way. Whatever has been done can be undone by a simple shifting of your mindset.

You don't have to live in defeat. You don't have to keep barely surviving from paycheck to paycheck. You can walk in true abundance. Choose to be a different kind of fruit on your family tree.

Are you willing to commit to this challenge? Are you willing to be bold enough to try what I am talking about? Will you have the courage to grab a mustard seed of faith and believe that things will get better if you actively work this system? If so, keep reading, because what lies on the rest of these pages reveal the secrets to financial freedom.

> ***Take the first step in faith. You don't have to see the whole staircase, just take the first step. —***
> Martin Luther King, Jr.

OBSERVE THE FACTS

Now that you have decided to commit to this challenge, the next step is to get real about your current financial situation. You have to evaluate the decisions you made with money in the past. Make a "T" chart on a piece of paper. On one side list all of your liabilities, and on the other side list all of your assets. The key is to find out exactly where you are now so that you can know how far away you are from your targeted financial goal. Start keeping a daily journal of what you spend your money on. Do this exercise for a full month. I am sure you will be amazed to find out where your money is really going.

FOCUS ON THE DESTINATION

We have been so conditioned to focus on the things that we don't want that we forget to focus on the things we do. We go through life reacting to what life brings us. I am a firm believer that what you focus on, you attract. You must get, and maintain, a clear mental picture of the financial goal(s) you are trying to reach. Otherwise, you will continue to wander around in circles achieving nothing.

I am reminded of the movie *Alice in Wonderland*. In one of the scenes from the movie, Alice came to the fork in the road and saw Cheshire the cat in a tree. "Which road do I take?" Alice asked. "Where do you want to go?" Cheshire the cat replied. "I don't know" Alice answered. "Then it doesn't matter which way you go," said the cat. In other words, Cheshire was trying to let her know that if she didn't know where she wanted to go, then any road would take her there. This story gives you a clear glimpse of how not knowing where you want to go can lead you down a road to nowhere. How can you ever expect to reach your destination if you don't know where you are going?

...not knowing where you want to go can lead...to nowhere.

CHOOSE TO NEVER BORROW MONEY AGAIN

Contrary to popular belief, you cannot borrow your way out of debt. Borrowing only leads you deeper and deeper into financial liability. Pay close attention to this sentence: borrowing money from someone automatically makes you a slave to them. Please, if you learn nothing else from reading this book, study this principle. This paragraph is worth reading again.

You must make the decision to never again borrow money (with the exception of purchasing a house). If you do not commit to a refusal to borrow, you will spend the rest of your life living under someone else's conditions.

> ***The rich ruleth over the poor, and the borrower is servant to the lender.* —**
>
> Proverbs 22:7

REASONS TO STOP BORROWING MONEY

Stop taking out consolidation loans, car loans, home equity loans, lines of credit, etc. I have watched people time and time again take out these loans. They pay the loan(s) off then turn around and go right back into debt. It's a vicious cycle. If only people would realize the bondage they are creating for their lives. If only they would stop and think about the real transaction that is taking place and how it is costing them their freedom.

In Joel Osteen's book, *Become a Better You*, he tells a story about a man who has several horses. One day one of the horses kicked a wooden fence and damaged its leg. The man took the horse to his barn and bandaged the leg. After a couple of weeks, he noticed that the horse's leg was not getting better. The man had a veterinarian come out and take a look at the horse. The vet prescribed some antibiotics and the horse responded to the medicine immediately and started to get better. After a month or two, the owner noticed that the horse's leg still hadn't healed. It actually began to get worse. So, the vet put the animal on the same medicine. Once again, the animal began to get better, but after a short time, the process repeated itself. The wound would not heal. Finally, the owner took the horse down to the veterinarian clinic. The veterinarian put the horse under anesthesia and began to probe the infected area on its leg. Low and behold, the veterinarian discovered a large piece of wood that had gone far below the skin where the horse had hit the fence a few months prior. The vet realized that every time the animal stop taking the antibiotic, the infection caused by that foreign object returned. They were only treating the symptoms instead of treating the true source of the problem.

...you have to determine that nothing will deter you...

There has to be a changing of your mindset. You have to stop bandaging the symptoms and fix the real problems that are keeping you from becoming financially fit. The benefits of changing your philosophy about debt will outweigh any sacrifice you may have to make. The people who are tired of quick fixes and who have their minds made up to do whatever it takes to be free from the bondage of debt are the people who will succeed in the long run.

DETERMINATION

In order to live a debt-free lifestyle, you have to determine that nothing will deter you from your goal. Believe me, there are going to be times when you will want to give up and throw in the towel. There will be times when you wonder why you even started this journey in the first place. You must keep your eyes focused on the ultimate prize—financial freedom. Trust me—it's worth the journey.

PERSEVERANCE

At TheFreeDictionary.com, perseverance is defined as "a steady persistence in adhering to a course of action, a belief, or a purpose." It is important to know that when you start something worthwhile, opposition will always come your way. The initial reaction is to give up or give in. But when you are focused and single-minded, nothing can stop you. Most people fail either before they start or right before they reach the end. Think back on a time when you achieved a major accomplishment. Did you not experience obstacles when you set out to realize one of your goals?

About a year ago, we counseled a married couple who were deep in debt. For as long as they had been married, they had never worked together as a couple on achieving their financial goals. When it came to budgeting, they thought they would be better off if they kept their finances separate. After trying it their way for several years, they realized that matters were only getting worse. So, they sought us out for help.

After working with them for two months, they found themselves continuing to make mistakes by overspending for the week. They immediately became discouraged, but I assured them that they were in the right place at the right time, and that making mistakes is a part of learning. A mistake lets you know that you have not stopped trying. They were making tremendous progress—they just could not see it at that moment as they could not see the forest for the trees as the old saying goes.

Think of newborn babies who have yet to develop their teeth. At first you have to feed them milk as they can't digest solid food. Over time, when they start to grow teeth, you can begin to wean them off of liquids and feed them solids. It is a development process. It takes time to change. The couple did not develop all of their bad financial habits in one day, so they would not be able to change them in one day. We just kept reminding them how far they had come within such a short period of time and encouraged them to keep moving forward.

They were right where they were supposed to be in their developmental stage. If you had talked to them a month prior, you would not have known that this was the same couple. In only two months, they were finally able to sit down and discuss their budget. Instead of arguing over their finances, they began to talk things out calmly and rationally. This was a major accomplishment for them. Over the next few months, they began to pay more attention to managing every dollar they spent. Every month they continued to get better and better at budgeting together. In less than a year of working with them, they are almost finished paying off all their debts, with the exception of their home. If they had not kept a positive attitude of perseverance, they would not be where they are today.

> ***The big secret in life is that there is no big secret. Whatever your goal, you can get there if you're willing to work.*** —
>
> Oprah Winfrey

EVERYONE EXPERIENCES HARD TIMES

In the beginning of our marriage, there were so many times when I questioned why I continued to keep Quaneshala and myself on a budget. This was especially true since I was still learning how to set financial goals as a couple. I had become accustomed to making all of the executive decisions about spending. Now that I was married, I had to learn how to listen to and respect my wife's vote in the decision making process. Honestly, it took some time to learn how to pay attention to her viewpoint. I'm still learning how to understand her many different styles of communication, as she knows how to express herself in so many ways. Each method that she chooses to communicate is a challenge for me to not mistakenly misinterpret what she is trying to convey. Once I began to accept and value her opinion, we were better able to move forward to accomplish our goals.

PROCRASTINATION

It's wise to forewarn you about one of the enemies of success, namely the enemy of ***procrastination***. Procrastination is a thief of success as well as a robber of time. It will cause you

Procrastination is a thief of success...

to miss out on all that life has to offer you. One way to overcome procrastination is to set goals that will keep you up late at night and cause you to rise early in the morning. Setting the right goals will cause you to become excited and motivate you to keep moving forward. If you find yourself procrastinating, review or rewrite your goals until you are excited about accomplishing them again.

> ***Procrastination is the bad habit of putting off until the day after tomorrow what should have been done the day before yesterday.*** —
> Napoleon Hill

SAYING THE RIGHT WORDS

Words have a way of shaping our lives in so many different ways. The words we use can dictate our future. For example, let's take three words that most of us use on a daily basis.

Could – you have the ability to perform the task
Should – you would consider performing the task
Have – you are committed to performing the task

The words you choose to use in your sentences reveal how serious you are about taking action. Let me explain further. Pretend that you needed to paint the house. If you said to me that you "could" do it, I would immediately know that you have the physical ability to paint. However, that doesn't mean that you are serious about completing the task. If you used the word "should" do it, I would then know that you understand this to be an important task, but other things are competing for your attention at the moment. At this level, it is more than likely that the painting is not going to get done any time soon. It may take years before you get back around to completing this task. The use of the word "have" will change the priority of your thinking. When you "have" to do something, you place the job on a high priority level.

The words we use can dictate our future.

When I hear clients say that they "have to get out of debt", I know that they are determined to do whatever it takes to become debt-free. It is now a major priority; nothing will stop them. Start consciously paying attention to the words you use every day as they have the potential to shape your future.

WHAT'S INFLUENCING YOU

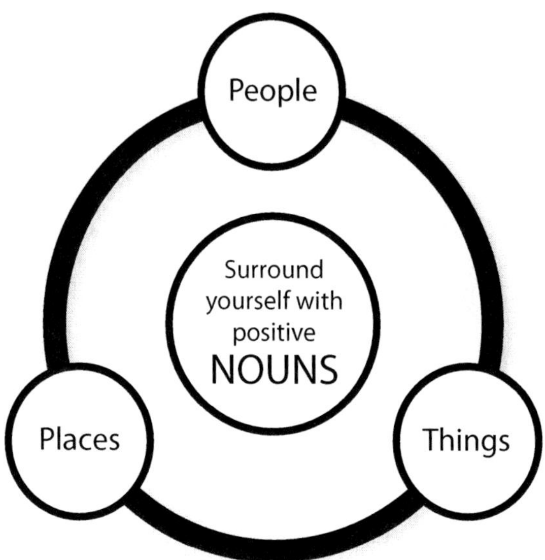

It is very important to surround yourself with positive NOUNS while you are reconditioning your mind to this new lifestyle. It would be contradictory to continue to hang out with the same people, go to the same places, or do the same things that caused you to get into financial bondage in the first place.

I'm certain that if you were trying to lose weight, you would not hang out at a bakery all day. If you did, failure would be inevitable. You cannot rely on *willpower* alone to help you accomplish everything. Willpower will only get you so far. Start setting up daily routines so that you will automatically choose the right people, places, and things to further your goals. For example, seek out people who are working towards the same financial objectives that you are. Start looking for places or events around town that have financial workshops. This is also a great place to meet like-minded people. Lastly, remove all the negative distractions (e.g. movies, television shows, books, news, etc.) from your life that contradict your new philosophy. Always keep your mind focused on the positive.

> ***Whatever you vividly imagine, ardently desire, sincerely believe, and enthusiastically act upon... must inevitably come to pass!*** —
>
> Paul J. Meyer

FOCUS WITH THE END IN MIND

Wake up every day with the end in mind. Think about how you will feel once you are financially free. Allow yourself the privilege to feel and express those emotions now. Don't cheat yourself like I once did. I used to rob myself out of so many victories and accomplishments in the past. I did not realize the importance of celebrating before and after an accomplishment. I used to always tell myself that there would be plenty of time to enjoy my victory after the final goal was accomplished. The problem with my method was that I never got around to celebrating once I finally achieved my goal. My only focus was to hurry up and start on my next one. I did not take time out to feel and enjoy my current victory.

I finally learned this principle in 2008 when I attended an *Unleash the Power Within* event by Anthony Robbins. It was an awesome conference. Tony used a fire walking exercise to teach us the importance of facing our fears head on and without hesitation. The fire walk alone was a great lesson in and of itself. The most important lesson I gained from this experience, however, was the significance of celebrating both big and small accomplishments. If you don't acknowledge *each* of your achievements, you won't be able to build the confidence you will need for the challenges ahead.

...celebrate both big and small accomplishments.

Think of it this way. Experts say that in order to reinforce positive behavior and eliminate negative behavior in children, it is imperative that you acknowledge and praise them every time they do something right. This conditions them to realize the importance of what they did at that very moment that caused you to praise them. Over time you will not have to worry about disruptive behavior because you are giving them attention for their positive actions.

On the other hand, what do you think would happen if you gave them positive feedback days or months later after the fact? What if you only focused on the things they did not do right? You will find that they will continue in wrongdoing because at least they are receiving some form of attention, regardless of the fact that it is negative.

PAYING ATTENTION MATTERS

Early in my teaching career, I had a student in one of my computer application classes whom I'll call Sandra. From the very beginning of the school year, she was absolutely one of my favorite students. I would personally speak to her every day as I spoke to all my students as they entered the room. She loved the extra attention I gave by calling on her to answer a question in class. She would also volunteer to sit at the demonstration computer during class.

Midway in the semester, I had a new student transfer into my class. I soon started to notice that Sandra began to disrupt the class by talking out loud and joking with friends across the room. This was the complete opposite behavior that she had shown me since the beginning of the semester. This pattern continued for about a week before I ended up having a meeting with her and her mother. Neither her mother nor I could figure out why she had started acting up in class all of a sudden. To make a long story short, I discovered that the reason for her disruption was because she believed that I was now giving all of my attention to the new student. After realizing this, I began to publicly acknowledge her when she exemplified the right behavior in class. In a matter of days, her behavior was back to normal.

KNOWING THE RISK

One day I had a conversation with a very good friend of mine who is an accomplished Certified Public Accountant. We spent over an hour debating questions about whether or not it was possible for individuals to live in a world without debt; good debt versus bad debt; and why/how companies use debt as a powerful tool for operational expenses. During our conversation, one of her comments stuck with me. It was when she tried to convince me that companies need a certain level of debt to operate successfully. Needless to say, I totally disagreed with her.

I only had three questions I wanted her opinion on. If debt

is such a powerful tool, how was Chase Bank able to purchase Washington Mutual Bank (WaMu) for pennies on the dollar? How do you think people felt when they lost their jobs and did not know how they were going to pay their bills? How do you think people felt when they had to foreclose on the home they had lived in for years?

I know that I am belaboring this point, but I want to be clear in my statement that debt is **not** your friend. Let me repeat that. ***Debt is not your friend***. If you are ever put into a position where you are unable to repay the lender, at that very moment you will find out how much the lender truly cares about you personally. For them, there is no emotional attachment: it's just business as usual. They only want their money back.

Debt is not your friend.

If you are reading this, please heed this warning. Don't wait until you have a financial crisis before you decide to free yourself from the bondage of debt. We have counseled so many people who thought they were able to manage the debt they had accumulated, but after they experienced an emergency (e.g. layoff, job loss, death), they had a hard reality to face. Please don't let tragedy strike before you decide to change your financial status.

SYMETRICE RODGER'S STORY

Symetrice and my wife have been friends for over 15 years. Before Symetrice got married, my wife always talked to her about the importance of paying off her bills and living a debt-free lifestyle. Symetrice appreciated the advice my wife gave her and began to implement changes in her spending to work towards obtaining financial freedom.

During their engagement, Symetrice persuaded her fiancé, Daryl, to agree on a plan for them to become debt-free in four years. They decided to pay cash for their wedding and begin their financial plan after the wedding.

After almost two years of successfully following their debt elimination plan, Symetrice started having headaches. After going to the doctor for a routine checkup, she found out that she had a tumor on the right side of her brain. After a series of tests from other doctors, they confirmed that it was indeed a tumor. After weighing her options on what actions to take next, she decided to have the tumor surgically removed.

After the surgery, the doctors were amazed at how well Symetrice brain was functioning. She was alert and well aware of her surroundings. Because of the seriousness of the operation, she was very thankful that she could still talk. She also did not suffer any memory loss. We were so happy to receive a phone call from her the day after the operation. It was miraculous being able to hear the excitement in her voice. She was truly happy and in good spirits.

The main reason I am including Symetrice story in this book is because of the astonishing attitude she had even when she first learned of her condition. After telling my wife the news, Symetrice could not stop thanking her for all of the advice my wife had given her over the years. Symetrice was so grateful that she and her husband were able to pay off a lot of debt before their health crisis happened. It was an empowering moment for them to be able to pay cash for her MRI's and doctor visits.

Although Symetrice has a long road of recuperation ahead of her, my wife and I believe God will provide for her total recovery. We are confident that her journey will be much easier now that she is financially prepared. Sickness is stressful enough without having to worry about one's financial stability, and we're grateful to have helped her eliminate some of that particular worry so she can focus on a speedy healing.

> ***All of the problems we're facing with debt are manmade problems. We created them. It's called fantasy economics. Fantasy economics only works in a fantasy world. It doesn't work in reality. —***
>
> Michele Bachmann

WE LIVE IN THE "WANT IT NOW" ERA

We live in a time of got to have it, got to get it, and got to enjoy it…NOW! I read an article the other day that reported on how people who once made millions are now living in poverty. It's very disappointing to hear about someone whose life drastically changed due to what I call an avoidable circumstance. How can you go from literally making millions to being homeless? You once had the finances that some can only dream of; now you have switched roles and have become the dreamer again. How did this happen?

CAN YOU AFFORD TO WIN?

When people ask me for advice on a certain financial risk they were getting ready to take, I always tell them, "If you can't afford to lose, you can't afford to win." Let me explain. I know that we can't live this life without taking any risk whatsoever. That's why it's called life. The important thing to know is that you can calculate the amount of risk you take. Don't just live your life by throwing up the cards and going with however they fall. A lot of people are so quick to make unwise decisions that it's scary to watch them in action. They think that planning to succeed is not important to living a happy and healthy life.

If you can't afford to lose, you can't afford to win.

If you ask people about the reasoning behind their decision for not planning, their response is that one has to have faith. I tell them that their faith must be mixed with a little bit of common sense. I personally don't know anyone who did not spend time mapping out a strategy before great success came their way. I also know a lot of people who did not plan and experienced great failure. Planning does not guarantee that you will not fail. Proper preparation will cause you to think about possible scenarios which will allow you to pick the best strategy. This will prevent you from wasting time and money on pitfalls that could have been avoided.

Planning does not guarantee that you will not fail.

ALMOST OUT OF GAS

One hot summer day, my wife and I were traveling from Mississippi to Florida. We were in a rental car so I kept forgetting to periodically check the gas gauge. We usually stop and refill the tank whenever we reach the quarter full mark. After being on the road for about four hours, I noticed that the gas light was on. We were almost out of gas! I suddenly jumped into panic mode. I slowed down to 55 mph, rolled down the windows and turned off the air conditioner to conserve fuel. I did not want to get stuck in the middle of nowhere on that hot summer day. You should have seen the two of us in that car. We started a powerful prayer meeting inside that box of steel. I know the people that passed us on the highway must have thought we were crazy!

A sign told us that the next gas station was 20 miles away. We did not know if we were going to make it that far. I knew that if the car ran out of gas, my wife would never let me forget it. After about 20 minutes of driving well below the speed limit and sweating in the heat, we arrived at a gas station. You can only imagine how relieved we were. I pulled up to the first available pump. I did not care what the price of gas was that day as I would have paid any amount at that point.

What would you have done in this situation? Ask yourself these questions: would you have stopped at the first available gas station, or would you have continued driving down the highway believing you could drive for another 50 miles before emptying the gas tank?

These questions may seem silly, but this scenario is the perfect example of how people manage their finances. We should not purposely put ourselves in harm's way and expect God to deliver us from our debt. The scripture instructs us not to tempt the Lord God. You may ask how one can tempt God financially. You tempt Him when you fail to plan for a rainy day knowing it's going to rain at some point in time. Life sends us different kinds of "seasons" that are just as predictable as autumn, winter, spring, and summer which occur here on earth. The average family will have at least one major emergency within a 10 year period. We know that the seasons of our lives are constantly changing. Let's choose to be wise in our actions and prepare for those seasons. This is real faith mixed with a little common sense. Please do have faith in God to bring you out because when He makes a way of escape known to you, take it.

Life sends us different kinds of "seasons" that are just as predictable as autumn, winter, spring, and summer...

> ***Be willing to be uncomfortable. Be comfortable being uncomfortable. It may get tough, but it's a small price to pay for living a dream. —***
>
> Peter McWilliams

GET UNCOMFORTABLE

We live in a society driven by comfort. We spend enormous amounts of money just to satisfy our need for pleasure. There is nothing wrong with enjoying a little bit of down time or fun. The problem comes when you find yourself indulging in it too often. Pleasure should be the exception, not the rule.

At this moment, are you living within your comfort zone? The lifestyle you live is a reflection of the level of comfort you enjoy. You have to decide how uncomfortable you are willing to become for the purpose of generating massive change. You will have to do what you have never done in order to get what you have never had. In other words, it involves stepping outside of your comfort zone. There are so many skills you can learn and develop if you are willing to set aside the time to master them.

Everything comes down to Your willingness to get uncomfortable in order to achieve your financial goals.

You may be thinking that you don't have enough time to commit to this change. In reality, there is always time to change if you desire to live the life of your dreams. You may have to rearrange your priorities to free up some of your time. Examine all the areas of your life where you waste time on unproductive activities (e.g. watching TV, playing video games, talking on the telephone, surfing the net, etc.) then replace them with actions that will help you achieve your goals.

Everything comes down to your willingness to get

uncomfortable in order to achieve your financial goals. Are you willing to cut some of the time you spend watching TV? Is that too big of a price to pay for success? Let's see what could happen if you reduced the time you spend watching television by one hour per day. You could spend that hour writing a page a day for a book on something that inspires you. In one year, you would have a 365 page book. You could literally become an author in a single year by choosing to write for one hour instead of watching television. Let's look at another example of using that hour wisely. Say you've had a gardening or "fix-it" project that you've been procrastinating in doing due to perceived lack of time. If you take those 60 minutes and apply yourself to repairing that leaky faucet or weeding your garden, you'll likely have that 'to do' job completed in one week!

Imagine freeing up more than just one hour each day by eliminating additional time-wasting activities. It would only be a matter of time before you achieved your ultimate financial dreams. Once again, it all depends on how uncomfortable you're willing to get. Are you willing to push past being uncomfortable in order to create the life you desire? You're the only one who can answer this question. Success will only come after your willingness to get uncomfortable expands.

> ***We all talk to ourselves. A major key to success exists in what we say to ourselves, which helps to shape our attitude and mindset.*** —
>
> Darren L. Johnson

NEW MINDSET

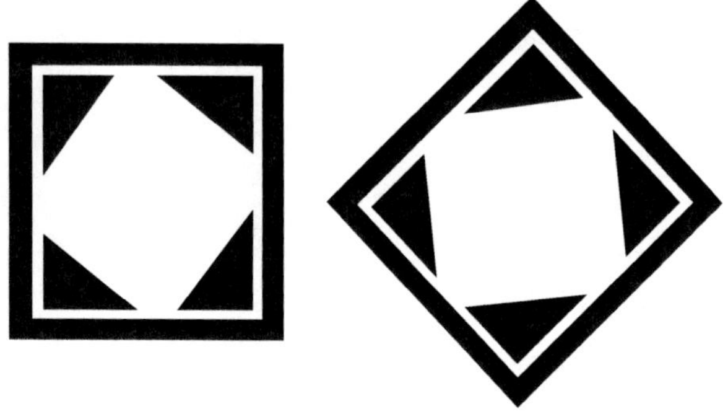

Examine the two shapes above carefully. What do you see on the left? If you said a square, you are correct. Now look at the shape on the right. What do you see? If you said a diamond, you are also correct. You may be wondering how both answers are correct when it is the same image. The reason is we interpret things in different ways. One person sees a square when another person sees a diamond. It's not a matter of who is right or wrong; it's a matter of how pessimistic or positive your outlook on life is. The choice is yours.

> ***By simply having a positive perspective on life, you can have a winning attitude...***

Do you see life as a stumbling block or as a rock-hard diamond that can easily slice through life's problems? If you pay close attention to these two figures, you will notice that they are exactly the same. The only difference between them is that one of them is turned 90° degrees. In most cases in life, there is always another option that you either fail to see or to notice, usually due to possessing a negative attitude. By simply having a positive perspective on life, you can have a winning attitude and a successful future. Go forward in life with the attitude that things are not always what they seem—they can even be better.

You may think your financial situation is beyond repair at first, but that is not the case. In spite of your initial feelings, just keep believing that things can and will get better. Continue to have faith that you will find the answer(s) you are searching for. Usually you will find that the correct course of action was right there in front of you all of the time. It just takes a closer view of the situation to form a new perspective. Make a shift in your thoughts and actions. If you will remove self out of the equation, God will always make a way.

5 EMOTIONAL STEPS TO SUCCESS

There are five emotional stages that everyone experiences when they set out to achieve success in any area. Even if you do not consciously become aware of them, you will have to experience each one before you achieve true success.

Inspired – This is usually the first emotional step you face when going after success. It involves creating excitement about a goal, causing you to believe within yourself that you could and should make a change.

Fear – Shortly after taking the necessary steps to commit and to achieve the desired goal, you begin to doubt your ability to accomplish it. As soon as you are faced with a challenging situation, the doubts assail. You constantly wonder whether you are good enough or talented enough. You may even fear what others will think of you if you succeed.

Self-Sabotage – Unconsciously you begin to revert back to your old patterns. You will start to prove to yourself that you are not good enough. Keep this truth close to your heart: whether you think you can or think you can't, you're correct!

Reflection – At this stage, you consciously become aware of past mistakes that keep you from reaching your goal. You recognize the ways in which you have self-sabotaged your life. You begin to review your goals and recommit to accomplishing them.

Total Confidence – When you experience this emotion you are 100% confident in yourself and in your abilities to obtain your desired goal. You know without a shadow of a doubt that you will succeed and not fail. You are willing to face and overcome any roadblocks that come your way.

If you keep moving through all of these stages, success will be sure to overtake you.

SHARING POVERTY

One day, I watched a story on TV that was featuring families who needed serious financial help. The host invited a well-known financial adviser to help each family overcome their financial struggles. One family, a mother and her two daughters, was seeking advice on how to help the younger sister overcome her major spending habit. They could not understand why the younger sister continually spent money she did not have. As a result, she continued to borrow money from her mother and from her older sister. She even pressured her older sister into co-signing a loan on a house that the younger sister could not afford. It had gotten to the point where the younger sister had spent all of her mother's savings. To make matters worse, the older sister did not have any extra money to spend on herself because she was constantly lending money to her younger sister.

Every time the mother and older sister tried to talk to the youngest sister about her spending habits, she would lay a guilt trip on them by saying that they didn't love her if they refused to loan her money. This went on for years without them challenging the younger sisters' accusations.

The turning point came one day when the younger sister asked her older sister to give her money so she could pay her house payment on time. The older sister took the money she had been saving up to buy an exercise machine and gave it to her younger sister. The older sister felt that she would delay her purchase in order to show her younger sister that she loved her. Plus, she had gotten used to bailing her younger sister out every time she asked for help financially.

Weeks later, the older sister found out that her younger sister had bought a flat screen TV with the money she had loaned her which was supposed to go towards the house payment. When she went over to her house to confront her, she discovered that her baby sister had made several other big ticket purchases. The straw that broke the camel's back, as the saying goes, was when she found out that one of those costly items was an exercise machine—the very item the older sister had postponed purchasing for the sake of helping her younger sister pay her mortgage. The older sister could not believe how her younger sister had taken advantage of her. So, the mother and the older sister finally said "No more!" and decided to seek help for their family.

After reviewing their story, the financial adviser gave the family some advice on how to rebuild their relationship, and how to set new boundaries with one another. The mother and older sister would have to start by discontinuing bailing out the younger sister every time she got into a financial crunch. She also explained to them that giving the younger sister money was not letting her share the family's wealth. In reality, the family was sharing the younger sister's poverty. The selfish sister was causing the family to suffer financially. The savings that the mother and older daughter once had were now depleted as they had allowed the younger sister to borrow money without paying it back.

After watching this show, I realized that this was not the only family experiencing this problem. Many others experience the same or similar problems. This same predicament could involve a sibling, a parent, a friend, or a spouse. You find yourself always helping them out because you have substituted real love with loaning them money. You are only hurting them by enabling them. This is a hard truth to accept because we have been taught that we must help others unconditionally. We probably feel, too, that they would help us if we found ourselves in the same dilemma.

Our human nature craves to help others.

Please don't misunderstand my point. You should want to help others. Our human nature craves to help others. My wife and I constantly donate our time and money to causes we believe in. You must choose, however, to give in a way that will build, strengthen, and encourage others to set a higher financial standard for their own lives. It's important that help is offered in a way that will cause them to boldly face their fears of achieving financial independence. Realize that money is not always the answer as usually it is just a quick fix. It would be much better if you teach a person how to fish so that they can eat for a lifetime as opposed to giving them a fish that will only feed them for one day.

USE THE WORD "NO"

I have personally told several people that I would not give them money if they were unwilling to take my financial advice to turn their situation around. This was especially true if they were coming to me with the same problem for the second time around. I don't have a problem saying no to people because I realize that quick fixes only hurt them in the long run. Sometimes it takes experiencing a little pain for people to change. Think about some of the hardest times in your life. At first I am sure your difficulties seemed like the worst moments you'd ever experienced. Nevertheless, those hard times yielded fruit because you learned so much during the trial. You found yourself growing and developing into a completely different person who was able to use the experience as a catalyst to make better decisions about your life and about your lifestyle. You are now able to help someone else who is going through the exact same thing you went through. We don't always understand the why's of life. I am convinced, though, that whatever we face in this life will work out for our ultimate good.

ARE YOU FEEDING A NEED WITHIN YOURSELF?

Look within yourself and make sure that you are not fulfilling your own selfish needs through giving. When I first started dating, I used to attract needy women who made me feel loved. I attracted these kinds of women because I did not grow up with my mother telling me that she loved me on a regular basis. She certainly showed her love by the things she did for my brothers and I, but the words were absent. Therefore, the women I dated drew me with their tender words, love, and care which in turn, made me feel needed. I then became an enabler. I ran to their rescue so I could hear those sweet words of love and encouragement. After running through these hoops over and over again, I finally faced the truth about what I was doing. I was letting my insecurities keep me from being in a healthy relationship. It was a hard change to make, but I'm glad I made it. This change helped me to find and marry a truly remarkable woman, and I'm happy to say that our relationship is very healthy and solid.

THE VALUABLE PENNY

Have you ever taken the time to look at and think about the value of a penny? At first glance, it seems like a penny is not a lot of money. There isn't much you can buy with it at its present value. People are constantly walking past pennies on the ground everyday because pennies are not regarded as anything valuable. If you are shortsighted, you agree with the previous statement as being true. But if you knew the power of compounding, you would probably have a different answer.

If you were given a choice between taking $2,000,000 in

cash this very instant or taking a single penny that doubles in value every day for 31 days, which would you choose? Most people would choose the $2,000,000 in a heartbeat. They would immediately begin to think about all the ways they could spend it. For those who chose the penny, let's take a look at what you will end up with within the next thirty days by your decision to delay pleasure.

In the first 10 days of your penny compounding, it would only be worth $5.12. I am sure your friends that chose the $2,000,000 would be laughing at you and wondering why you did not take lump sum payment and run like they did. They would be parading their new toys and trinkets around you which just might cause you to doubt your decision. But let's continue the story to see what happens next. On day 20, your penny would now be worth $5,242. It's possible that now you are beginning to worry because you only have 11 days left to increase your initial investment. You're probably thinking that there is no way you will be able to catch up with your friend's choice of $2,000,000. And you're right. What exactly will you have in the end?

Wait! Don't give up now! Please don't waste all the time and hard work you put into watching your penny grow. On day 31, you will have a total of $10,737,418. That's 5 times more than the initial $2,000,000 offered at the beginning of this example. I'm sure you want to know how this is possible. Well, that is the power of compound interest. Albert Einstein called it the eighth wonder of the world. This is the number one reason why individuals should start investing as early and as young as possible. We will talk more about investing in a later chapter.

Day	Amount	Day	Amount
1	$0.01	17	$655.36
2	$0.02	18	$1,310.72
3	$0.04	19	$2,621.44
4	$0.08	20	$5,242.88
5	$0.16	21	$10,485.76
6	$0.32	22	$20,971.52
7	$0.64	23	$41,943.04
8	$1.28	24	$83,886.08
9	$2.56	25	$167,772.16
10	$5.12	26	$335,544.32
11	$10.24	27	$671,088.64
12	$20.48	28	$1,342,177.28
13	$40.96	29	$2,684,354.56
14	$81.92	30	$5,368,709.12
15	$163.84	31	$10,737,418.24
16	$327.68		

Compound interest is the eighth wonder of the world. He who understands it, earns it... he who doesn't...pays it. —

Albert Einstein

MOVING FORWARD WITHOUT LOOKING BACK

Andy Andrews, an author and motivational speaker, tells a story about Hernán Cortés, a Spanish Conquistador, who traveled to Mexico in search of the world's richest treasure. This bounty had laid in obscurity for over 600 years. Before they set sail, he gathered his troops and inspired them with a story of how their life would be after finding the treasure.

When they finally reached the New World, the troops were restless and eager to find the gold. He assembled his men and gave them one last order: "Burn the boats." Cortés knew that in order for them to be successful in finding the treasure, he had to eliminate any and all back-up options for failure.

This is a remarkable story because it points out one very important characteristic of what one must have to achieve great things. You must possess the ability to take away all options of retreat. When you begin this new debt-free lifestyle, it is very important to walk into it with an attitude of confidence and a certainty of success. If you go into this with a half-hearted approach, you are destined to fail. It's possible to find yourself worse off than ever, as though you did not even make an attempt at all. Before moving on to the second level of this book, take a moment right now and decide that you will take the necessary actions required to obtain your desired outcome. Determine that this will be the first day of the rest of your life.

GROW OR DIE

Now that you are equipped with the knowledge on how to start along the path to financial success, reinforce the principles you have learned by practicing your newly developed habits daily. You must continue to grow by finding things that will add value to your life and that will help bring you closer to your financial destiny. Remember, surrounding yourself with positive nouns/words (e.g. books and audio recordings) will encourage you during the working of your plan.

Have you ever seen a person who committed themselves to change, but within months ended right back where they started? The reason is because they did not realize that they had to continue to condition their mind for success every day. We are the sum total of all the decisions we made in the past. Better said, all of the decisions made today affects tomorrow. Want a better tomorrow? Change your today.

The good news is that transformation can happen in an instant. Many people get discouraged because the manifestation of their hopes, dreams, and desires do not happen all at once. Keep having faith. Know and believe that once you take massive action, the intangible will soon become tangible. Otherwise, you will be tempted to fall back into your old, unproductive patterns which will inevitably lead you back to your beginning point. Patience is the key to sustainable success. Don't worry; soon you will achieve the results you have been anticipating.

> ***Life is change. Growth is optional.***
>
> ***Choose wisely.* —**
>
> Karen Kaiser Clark

LEVEL 2:
GET REAL

Now that you have decided to transform your life around and make a 180° turn in the opposite direction, you are ready for the 2nd level of financial freedom. In this level, we will take an honest look at your current financial situation. You will begin to craft a workable financial freedom action plan to use for the rest of your life. You will now start to see that you are in control of creating your own reality.

BE HONEST

First you must start by being honest about your situation. Honesty is the best way to total recovery. You have to take a sober look at where you are and the actions that lead to this point in your life. What were the triggers that made you over spend? Ask yourself questions like:

- ❏ Who did I learn my financial habits from?
- ❏ What sense of enjoyment do I receive by spending money I don't have?
- ❏ Do I spend money when I have a stressful day?
- ❏ Do I spend money instead of dealing with my emotions?
- ❏ Do I plan out a budget before I make purchases?

By asking yourself hard questions such as these will cause you to pay more attention to why you spend as you do. Here is an example. If you know that you spend more money whenever you go to the grocery store on an empty stomach, try eating before you go shopping. Another suggestion is to make a list of items that you need before leaving home. If the item is not on your list, don't put it into your shopping cart.

You can find a way to eliminate bad spending.

By developing these habits, you will begin to teach yourself discipline. There are a number of things you can do to replace your bad habits with good habits. Trust me; there is nothing new under sun. You can find a way to eliminate bad spending habits. Many people have been faced with the same challenges you are now experiencing and still met with success. The major difference between them and you is that they kept trying until they found a system that worked best for them. It is not a question of if you can do it, but will you do it?

You are where you are because of your past actions. The best part about that last sentence is that as soon as you start taking different steps in a different direction, you will start becoming the person you desire to be. Think about it this way. Sometimes a person is only overweight because of the bad food choices that were made in the past. Once they begin to make better food choices and exercise, their body will begin to change almost immediately. It will of course take some time before the true results of their efforts are revealed. This is especially true if they have been overeating for years. As long as the new lifestyle is maintained, it will only be a matter of time before their weight loss goal is reached. The exact same principle applies to your finances. You may have been down in a financial hole, but you now own a shovel (this book)! Dig yourself out of that hole and move on to a life of wealth and abundance!

> ***I am the master of my fate,***
> ***I am the captain of my soul. —***
> William Ernest Henley

ACCEPTANCE

Accept where you are right now. Recognize the fact that you have made some bad financial decisions in the past. But don't stop there. Accept that things have already started to change for the better. Believing in YOU will make all the difference in the world—your world. I've already stressed earlier in the book that you need to let this be a fresh start for you. Take the approach that this is your new life and nothing can stop you.

CONSUMER EQUITY SHEET

Take out a piece of paper and draw a vertical line down the middle of the paper. Draw a horizontal line 1/3 from the top of the page. The lines should form a T. On the left side, write Assets. This should include all the things you own. On the other side of the page, write down your Debts. This side should include all the banks, credit card/loan companies, family, friends, and people to whom you owe money.

Now, total the numbers on each side. Then subtract your total assets from your debts. Is the number positive or negative? If it is positive, that's great. You are off to a great start. If the number is negative, don't worry. This is the exact same situation I started with. As you begin to work this system, your liabilities will begin to decrease while your assets will begin to increase.

Deceive yourself no more about your financial state.

Writing down all of your assets and debts will serve as a snapshot of your current financial condition. You must know where you are financially in order to know where you are going financially. Deceive yourself no more about your financial state. The truth is right there on the paper in black and white. It's time to face your fears.

You perhaps have become fearful after completing this exercise. Maybe the numbers are not adding up the way you expected them to. But fear is unnecessary because God has not given us the spirit of fear. Fear only shows up when we think we cannot change our situation or when we think we have no control over our life.

After the children of Israel left Egypt, God told them to go in and possess the land that He had promised to them. Moses sent twelve spies to scout out the land. When they came back, no one could deny that the land was everything that God said it would be. It was a place flowing with milk and honey. The fear came when they saw the giants who were currently residing in the land. The children of Israel saw themselves as grasshoppers compared to the giants. Their fear caused them to miss out on the blessings that God had provided just for them. Israel's failure to possess the land God gave them caused them to wandering around in the wilderness for forty years. The rest is history.

Since you are reading this book, you know that this is your time to take action. I know, I know. You feel that fear is a natural part of life. You're certainly right, but don't give fear any power over you. Don't let fear keep you from being free. I believe that before you began reading this book you would have run away from your giants. Not anymore. You possess the faith and courage to press onwards to win the prize.

...don't give fear any power over you.

Again, don't worry about how things are going to work out. Stop trying to figure out the entire picture. Take it one day at a time. Focus on financial success each day. Before you know it, the days will have turned into weeks, the weeks into months, and the months into years.

> ***The only way to get anything is to get it done. —***
> Anonymous

PURPOSE OF A BUDGET

I did not use a budget when I first moved to Texas and started living on my own. I thought I was smart enough to remember the math in my head. I planned to spend every penny I earned. If I had any money left over at the end of the month, I considered myself a failure for not wasting more money on things I did not need. It was not until the summer of 2005 (3 ½ years later), when I discovered what a budget was all about. The purpose of a budget is to help you turn your financial goals into reality (I will talk more about goals in a later section). For instance, if one of your goals was to save $1,000,000 for retirement, yet you are not currently saving any money, it's highly unlikely that you will retire with that goal met. It's like planting carrot seeds, but expecting a harvest of oranges.

BUDGETING

Yeah, I know what you're thinking. "Why do I need to prepare a budget? I hate budgets. There is no fun and freedom in budgets." Well, starting out it may seem that way. A budget directs your use of money. It teaches you how to spend money and what to spend it on. A budget helps you to develop in the area of discipline. You learn to say "no" to yourself when you are tempted to spend too much. You want to know exactly where every dollar is going before you spend it.

Think of planning a budget in the sense of planning a vacation. You would not leave the country without first making a list of needed items. It's the same with budgeting. You should not spend your paycheck without knowing where every physical dollar is going. Use the sample categories chart below to guide you in creating your budget.

Sample Categories Chart				
Housing	**Food**	**Transportation**	**Personal Care**	**Children**
Mortgage/Rent Phone Electricity Gas Water/Sewer Cable Waste Removal Maintenance/ Repairs Supplies	Groceries Dining Out	Vehicle Payment Bus/Taxi Fare Insurance Licensing Fuel Maintenance/ Repairs	Allowance (His/Her) Hair/Nails Clothing Dry Cleaning Health Club Dues Toys/Games	Medical Clothing School Tuition School Supplies Dues Lunch money Child Care
Entertainment	**Savings & Investments**	**Gifts & Donations**	**Loans**	**Other**
Video/DVD's CD's Movies Concerts Sporting Events Live Theater	Retirement Account Investment Account Bank Savings College	Tithes Offering Charity Birthday Holidays	Personal Student Credit Card Store Card	Pets Legal

The first few months of learning how to budget, you are going to either overspend or under-spend on different categories in the budget. That's perfectly fine. It usually takes about three months of practice to stay on track with your budget. When emergencies arise, don't panic. Adjust your budget. The famous motivational speaker, Zig Ziglar, said, "Anything worth doing is worth doing poorly until you learn to do it well."

Time itself will make it easier...to stick to your budget

Time itself will make it easier and easier to stick to your budget. After a while you will see that spending every dollar before you get it will completely eliminate overspending. You will consciously know when you can or cannot afford an item. If it is not in your budget, you cannot make the purchase. Say goodbye to careless spending.

A budget gives you a way to plan for the upcoming week/month. Take a look at where you are spending your money. Think about who you are working for. I know you're saying, "I work for myself." Well, I hope that is the case. One look at your budget will immediately reveal whether or not your statement is true. If all of your money is being spent at Walmart, I will naturally assume that you are working for Walmart. The point is not that you should not buy anything from Walmart; the point is for you to wake up and realize the value and importance of keeping some of your money in your possession. Otherwise, you will in actuality be working for someone else.

> ***A budget is telling your money where to go instead of wondering where it went.*** — John Maxwell

THERE IS ROOM FOR ENJOYMENT

Of course you will be able to spend money on yourself again! I am not trying to take away your spending pleasure. I am only suggesting that you plan your purchases instead of just carelessly spending. A budget helps regulate the amount of money and the frequency with which you indulge. A budget only works if you work it.

THE EVALUATION PROCESS

After completing your budget, you may discover that you have a negative balance which leaves you wondering how you even survived this far. Writing your spending habits down on paper will give you a new perspective on how you're actually spending your money compared to how you thought you were spending it.

Now it's time to review your list and scrutinize each category. It's time to figure out how to minimize expenses and/or how to increase income. This process will teach you how to look for any and all ways to save money. If you are trying to get out of debt, you may have to drastically cut your expenses (we will talk more about how you will use the extra money to get out of debt in the Mountain Climbers section). Go through and eliminate items on your budget that you no longer need.

I have included a list of suggestions to help you save and/or increase your income.

WAYS TO SAVE ON YOUR BUDGET

Housing

- Rent for a cheaper rate, downsize your home
- Switch electric companies
- Switch to high efficiency light bulbs
- Bundle phone, Internet, cell phone, and cable (e.g. cancel cable or downsize on cell plans)

Food

- Buy in bulk
- Buy store brand versus name brand items
- Pack a lunch for work
- Substitute expensive ingredients in recipes
- Coupons (only on items you would have bought anyway)

Transportation

- Change car oil yourself
- Use regular gas instead of premium
- Drive a car that gets better gas mileage

Personal

- Buy off-season
- Shop the clearance rack
- Wear shoes and clothes longer
- Do your own manicures/pedicures/hair
- Look for beauty schools that provide discount services

Children

- Pack their lunch
- Limit eating out
- Shop at consignment stores
- Let grandparents keep children instead of daycare
- Find a job that allows you to work from home while children are small
- Give them an allowance for a set amount of chores (e.g. taking out the trash, cleaning their room)
- Let children spend their allowance to buy things they want

Entertainment

- Attend free events (e.g. live concerts, plays)
- Use coupons (e.g. 15% off, buy one/get one free)
- Eat at restaurants during lunch time (prices increase during dinner hours)

Savings & Investments

- Stop all contributions temporarily while paying off debt (we will discuss this more in the Mountain Climbers section).

Gifts & Donations

- Handmade crafts instead of expensive toys
- Coupons for service (e.g. free car wash, babysitting)

Loans

- Debt Elimination (will discuss in a later section)
- Search for credit cards with lower interest rates (only if present interest rate is extremely high)

Other

- Shop for bargains
- Walk the dog yourself
- Get better deals with cash
- Look for price match or BOGOF
- Give your dog a shampoo at home

Ways to Increase Income

- Wash cars
- Pray for pay increase
- Get a part-time job
- Start a side business
- Garage sales & eBay
- Adjust your tax withholding (only if you usually receive a tax refund at the end of the year)
- Focus daily on your financial goals
- Mow lawns
- Babysitting
- House sitting

BUDGETING FOR THE FIRST TIME

I remember when I first began budgeting. The main category I had problems with was the grocery fund. It took several months for me to get this category under control. I planned every meal; I took my lunch to work, and I ate breakfast and dinner at home. For the first two months, I still found myself running out of money before the month was over. I soon made the connection. I had grown accustomed to eating out. This left me spending less on groceries in the past. Armed with this knowledge, I adjusted the grocery allowance to reflect the fact that

I was eating at home more often. Although I had to make an adjustment to the grocery money budget, I was still able to save money by limiting the number of times I chose to eat out.

If you have not been keeping up with your spending in the past, budgeting will perhaps take a little time to get used to. You will find that some months will run smoothly while unexpected expenses will come up at other times. In the event that an unexpected expense does pop up, take a little time to consider the situation. Is it a major expense or can it be taken care of by swapping money from another category?

...budgeting will perhaps take a little time to get used to.

One year I had several family members desiring to come for a visit. I was excited about spending time with them, but at the same time, I did not want their visit to stop my debt-paying momentum. I looked over my budget and realized that I did not want to pull any money from my emergency fund. I was using the extra money I earned from working overtime at school to pay down my debts so I wasn't enthusiastic about the thought of putting my extra funds toward this unexpected expense. My final decision was to use money from my entertainment category to cover the additional costs of hosting my visitors. Everything worked out perfectly and we had a great time. More importantly, I did not have to sacrifice any of my goals in order to enjoy my family's visit.

LETTING GO CAN SEEM HARD

One of the hardest things for our clients to do is to adjust their budget. Usually they want change without giving up anything. We have to continually remind them not to focus on what they think they're losing, but instead stay in hot pursuit of the new and improved lifestyle that is possible for them.

Financial success is born of sacrifice. What you are willing to sacrifice determines how fast you become financially free. Do you want your sacrifice to be as painless as possible? Most likely your answer will be yes. However, the less you sacrifice, the longer it will take for you to reach your financial goals. I do have good news, though. The changes you make in the right direction today will put you in a better place than you were at yesterday. I don't want you to play around with your financial goals. What a tragic waste it will be for you to wake up ten years from now only to realize that you're in the same debt that could have been eliminated in only three years.

Financial success is born of sacrifice.

Start small if making big sacrifices seems to be too much too soon. Each month, try to save a little bit more than you did in the previous month. This method develops the habit of making sacrifices. Over time you will find it extremely easy to reduce your expenses.

RETHINK WHAT'S POSSIBLE

A couple of years ago I read a story about a family of seven living successfully on a modest income. Their story was nothing less than incredible. This family made wise use of their resources. They maximize every $1 they have. Reading their story will provoke you to rethink what's possible for your life.

AMERICA'S CHEAPEST FAMILY

While looking at the Today Show several years ago, I saw an unbelievable story about a family of 7 and how they live on a modest income. Mr. & Mrs. Steve Economides and their 5 children lived off of an annual income of about $44,000. The most impressive part is how much they were able to accomplish by living below their means. In nine years, they paid off their first house on an average income of $33,000. Their second home was purchased for more than $200,000 and is almost paid off. It is estimated to be worth more than $700,000. Their budget is broken down into 19 categories. They plan every meal before going to the grocery store by building their menu around specials and coupons. They wear nice clothes and buy late-model used cars with cash. They make purchases without using credit.

I hope their story inspires you to make the same smart decisions that this family has made over the years. Even though this is a condensed version of their story, you can nevertheless see how spending money the right way can have a major impact on someone's life. It will be worth your time to read their full story online at www.AmericasCheapestFamily.com.

GET YOUR INCOME UP

You might feel that reducing your budget is not the answer because you are barely making ends meet right now. Well, if that is the case, your only other option is to raise your income. This is not impossible to do. I'll share my story of how I accomplished this with you.

In 2005, when I first began to take control of my finances, I had to contemplate how I was going to pay off the mountain of debt I had accumulated. One of my first thoughts was to cease tithing until I eliminated debt. This initially seemed like an excellent idea until my strong Christian beliefs surfaced. I suddenly had thoughts of asking God for the money. I decided to ask God for an additional $20,000 for the coming year. This was indeed a big step of faith on my part. I had no way of knowing how God was going to manifest that money. I could only trust that my prayer would be answered.

We will fast forward to the end of the year. After tallying up my income for the past 12 months, I discovered that I had indeed reached my goal. It was actually easier than I had originally expected. This is not to imply that I did not work hard. We cannot be lazy and expect God to do all the work for us. When opportunities came for me to make extra money, I jumped onboard. I continued to do extra work within my school district throughout the year. This was God's answer to my prayer. God rewards productivity. He gives to each of us according to our ability as recorded in Matthew 25:14-29.

> ***But thou shalt remember the LORD thy God: for it is He that giveth thee power to get wealth, that He may establish His covenant which He swore unto thy fathers, as it is this day. —***
>
> Deuteronomy 8:18

GETTING CREATIVE: WAYS TO INCREASE YOUR INCOME

My wife told me about a child she saw on the news who was talking about how he made $50,000 cutting grass. His story began one day when he asked his mother for a few dollars. Times were tough and she didn't have the extra money to spare, so the boy started cutting grass to make a little extra money. I'm sure when he started this venture that success of this magnitude didn't enter his mind. Then he was eventually able to pay cash for a used truck which enabled him to haul around his lawn equipment. The story gets better as he even employed some of his high school friends for the summer to increase his business.

The above story is a great example of someone using creativity to improve his own life. Sure, he could have sat around complaining about his mom not being able to give him any money. Instead, he took matters into his own hands and started to create his own wealth. By taking the initiative, he restored his customers' beautiful yards, provided his friends with a nice paying summer job, and padded his pockets with extra cash.

CHANGE YOUR MINDSET

One of our clients, an entrepreneur, was struggling to grow her business and produce a profit. During one of our sessions, we suggested that she start thinking positively. We advised her to constantly ask herself throughout the day how she could make her situation better. I encouraged her to surround herself with positive "nouns": people, places, and things. (I talked about this in Level 1). I suggested that she start hanging around positive people. She also abstained from visiting negative places and started watching movies like *The Secret* in order to stay motivated. By changing her nouns, she averted her attention away from the situations she could not change and turned her focus onto the things she could.

After about a week, her thinking began to change. She wrote a check out to herself for $6,000 which represented the income she wanted to start receiving on a monthly basis. On her next paycheck, she did not get the $6,000 she had hoped for, she received $10,000! That's right! She earned $10,000 in commission for the month. Wait, there's more. She was rewarded an additional $10,000 for the month because she had increased her sales by 40% from the previous year. That's a total of $20,000. Not too shabby a return for simply changing her nouns, is it?

What changed for her? Did the economy change? No. The economy was the same as it had been for the past couple of years. Did the TV, radio, or mail advertisements generate the extra income? It probably played a part, but my client had been advertising for years and never achieved that much success. What changed was her attitude. She began looking for ways to make her situation better instead of finding all of the reasons why she was not succeeding.

TRAINED TO SPEND

If you have been a victim of impulse buying, please do not think there is something wrong with you. Advertisers are paid millions of dollars to figure out ways to get you to buy their products. They have spent years studying the purchasing habits of the masses. The sad truth is that they know you better than you know yourself. They have engineered your shopping habits down to a science. They know how bright to make the lights to draw you into their stores. Those wonderful scents you smell in their atmosphere are not accidental. Even the music shoppers hear playing in the background has been pre-determined.

...retailers purposely make it convenient for consumers to spend more money...

We have all had the experience of going into a store to purchase one thing only to leave that same store with a basket full of items we had no intention of buying. Again, there is nothing wrong with you. You do need to know, however, that retailers purposely make it convenient for consumers to spend more money than they really intended to when entering the store. We know their strategy is working well. Look at the large number of people facing financial trouble. Retailers are not going to stop using their strategies—because they work! Consumers must therefore use their own tactics to meet their financial goals. One strategy we personally use is called the Envelope System.

THE ENVELOPE SYSTEM

The Envelope System is designed to help you manage money in areas where you typically overspend. This system will keep you from making impulse purchases. If you walk into a store with $10.00, you are only going to walk out with $10.00 worth of merchandise – unless you stole it. It's a proven fact that people tend to spend more money when purchasing items with a credit card. This is because you do not consciously see and feel the money leaving your hand. Your brain does not register the fact that a transaction took place. It only detects that you are sliding your card and walking away with the item in your hand. No emotional attachment is involved. It feels as though you got something for free.

This is how the envelope system works. Look over your budget, make a list of all items for which you overspend, and total it up. When you receive your paycheck, go to the bank and take the exact amount in your budget out in cash. The idea is to start paying for each item on your list with cash from now on. One item on my list that I pay for with cash is entertainment. Every month, I go to the bank and take out $154 and put it into an envelope. We use this money for our "fun" money. I write *Entertainment Fund* on an index card and attach the index card and the money for that fund together with a paper clip and place it into an envelope.

Sometimes I divide the $154 into 4 weeks ($38 per week) and only spend that amount each week. There have also been times when we have spent the whole $154 dollars on one event during that month. Whether we spend the money over the course of a month or spend it all in one day, when the money is gone, it's gone. We do not go back to the bank for more cash. We learn to do without until the next month. When the next month rolls around, we start the cycle all over again.

Envelope System	
Entertainment	$154
Groceries	$300
Gifts	$100
Total	**$554**

The key to this system is to never spend more than what you've budgeted for and set aside in the envelope. If an unexpected emergency arises, figure out which other category you can "borrow" the money from rather than running to the bank to withdraw more cash or use your credit card. The old phrase "I'll use it (credit card) just this once" can quickly escalate into more frequent bouts of spending.

Remember: pay everything in cash only!

> *Some men have thousands of reasons why they cannot do what they want to, when all they need is one reason why they can. —*
>
> Mary Frances Berry

LEVEL 3:
TAKE ACTION

Building wealth is a process. It is not practical to try to learn and apply everything you gain knowledge of in one day. Your values and opinions will depend mostly on the phase you are going through in life. For example, a high school student will have different values and concerns than an adult with children. For this reason, I divided Level 3 into 4 major sections.

1. **Future Stars** – teach teenagers and college students how to make wise financial decisions
2. **Mountain Climbers** – for individuals needing to eliminate debt rapidly
3. **Trend Setters** – for individuals who are ready to experience the true meaning of financial freedom.
4. **Staying Together** – for engaged and married couples seeking to become one, or unified, in handling their finances

My primary focus is to impart the most important material for a person to use in relation to his/her current phase in life. It is therefore imperative to read all strategies outlined in each section because you will find valuable information in each one. So, please don't skip around assuming that you already know what the other sections are all about. You'll only end up short-changing yourself of life altering knowledge.

FUTURE STARS

I made it known in previous sections that I did not have a clue how to manage money. I was taught everything about transitioning into adulthood, except the knowledge, wisdom, and strategies needed to accomplish financial independence. Due to a lot of personal financial failures over the years, I have developed a passion to help teenagers and college students make smart financial decisions. My heart especially goes out to the college students who graduate with huge student loan debt only to spend years struggling to pay it off. There has to be a change and a better way to educate our youth. We have to reach the younger generations and show them how to prevent making the same financial mistakes we made in the past.

A Lesson of Value

Let's begin our first lesson with appreciate versus depreciate. Appreciate means to increase in value. In other words, something will be worth more over time. Some examples of items that will appreciate are Certificate of Deposit (CD's), investments, jewelry, antiques, paintings, sculptures, autographs, and real estate; usually anything that is scarce and valued by a large group of people.

The lesson here is to learn not to spend all our money on things that go down in value.

Depreciate means to lessen in value or price. Some examples of things that go down in value are clothing, motorcycles, computers, electronic equipment, consumables, cars, and furniture. Although there are some exceptions to both lists, for the most part this is an accurate list of things that can increase and decrease in value. The lesson here is to learn not to spend all your money on things that go down in value. It will be extremely hard to build wealth if you consistently buy things that depreciate with time. In short, you are not building equity in these types of possessions.

Buying a Car

A popular question that consumes the minds of high school students is, "Should I buy a new car?" This is especially true for college graduates. It is very tempting to run out and buy a new car with your first paycheck. It is important to realize that purchasing your first car should not be taken lightly as there is a lot to consider. For starters, let's examine the difference between financing new and used cars.

It is very tempting to run out and buy a new car with your first paycheck.

New car values fall an average of 60% within the first 4–5 years of the car's life. This means you will only have 40% of your investment in 5 years. Think of it this way. Pretend you gave me a $100,000 check to keep for you. You retrieve the money from me after five years. If I only gave you a $40,000 check because I spent the rest, I am sure you would be highly upset. Would this be a good deal? Yes, for me it would. I know this is an extreme example, but this is a general idea of how the depreciation of vehicles works. They are shiny and a lot of fun to drive, but is it really a wise investment? The following is a real-life example.

Person A spent $34,000 on a brand new 2011 Lexus IS 250. Five years later, that car would be worth somewhere around $21,000. In 10 years, it would probably be worth somewhere around $9,000. That's $25,000 of your money you will have lost in only 10 years. I would hate to even think about what this car would be worth in 20 years. My guess is that it would be worth very little.

Person B had the same $34,000 but bought a used 2007 Lexus IS 250 with 54,000 miles for around $21,000. By most people's standards, this would still be considered a fairly new car. If you took the leftover $13,000 and invested it at an 11% rate of return, in five years it would have grown to $22,476. In 10 years, your investment would be worth $38,859. For the sake of argument, would you believe me if I told you that in yet another 10 years, this same investment would be worth over $100,000? If you answered in the affirmative, you are correct. In a total of 20 years, this investment could grow to over $116,155.

Do you think Person A or Person B made the wiser decision? Person B, of course, made the wiser choice. Person B was able to "Kill two birds with one stone," as the saying goes. They were able to drive a nice car while still investing for the future.

I am not against buying new cars. My only concern is that you maximize every dollar you earn while you're still young. Trust me, if you apply the principles you learn in this book early on in your life, you will have plenty of time and money to purchase a new car later on if your heart so desires. Starting out, however, it's best that you focus on buying used cars until you've had time to build up a fair amount of assets. I will talk about this in more detail in the Trend Setters section. Remember: if you sacrifice a few desires now, you can obtain the

...if you sacrifice a few desires now, you can obtain the promise of living financially free later.

promise of living financially free later. So, do what you have to do as quickly as you can so you can do what you want to do as long as you can.

No Car Payment For Me

If you think you have to spend a lot of money or have a car payment in order to own a decent car, think again. When Christa decided to purchase a reliable car to take her from point A to point B, she settled on a 1990 Toyota Corolla. The best part about her decision is she only paid $400 for it. It was not fancy and did not have any of the latest bells and whistles. Truth be told, it could have been mistaken for an abandoned car. I could only laugh when she told us how she used to leave the keys inside the ashtray because she figured no one would steal it. She faithfully drove her car around the Dallas/Fort Worth area for a total of three years.

Most people thought she was crazy for buying such an old car especially since she was a single woman. They were worried about her someday being stranded on the highway. Christa did not pay any attention to her family and friends comments about her eighteen-plus year-old car. Over a three-year period, she only had to perform routine maintenance on the car (e.g. oil changes, brake service). She was aware of the car's main purpose—transportation, not style. Her focus was on using her money for items that appreciate in value. Her mind was set on building wealth. She sold her Corolla in 2011 for about the same amount of money she purchased it for three years prior.

Now she drives a 1997 Ford Taurus she bought for $1,000. If she continues this practice, I will not be surprised to find she has become a millionaire before her retirement.

Something to Think About

Before his death, Sam Walton, founder and owner of Walmart, was the richest man alive. He wore clothes from his own discount store and drove around in a pickup truck. I know we believe in having cars for status, but there is a lesson to be learned from how he lived his life. I seriously doubt if he was the least bit concerned of what others thought about him. If you want to be wealthy, you have to listen, watch, and do what wealthy people do. On the other hand, if you want to be broke, listen, watch, and do the things that broke people do. Albert Einstein defined insanity as "doing the same thing over and over again and expecting different results." Make no mistake about it: if you want to build wealth and keep it, you will have to think and act like a wealthy person. The next time someone gives you advice about how to achieve financial success, check their track record. You should clearly be able to see whether or not they have taken their own advice.

...if you want to build wealth and keep it, you will have to think and act like a wealthy person.

> ***It is always the start that requires the greatest effort.*** —
>
> James Cash Penney

Start Early on Retirement

We are going to talk more in detail about saving for retirement later in the TREND SETTING section. But at this juncture, I want to discuss the importance of starting an investment account in your tender years. Time is the #1 key advantage you have on a lot of other people. It is important to begin thinking about retirement while you are young. I know it may seem as if retirement is a thousand years away, but if you ask someone who is either retired or approaching retirement, they will all tell you the same thing: they wished they had planned for their retirement earlier.

Review the following chart. You will notice that Alvin started investing early at the age of twenty. He invested $1,200 a year ($100 a month), for ten consecutive years at an interest rate of 12%. After the 10th year, he stopped making contributions. Simon, another man the same age as Alvin, thought it would be okay to wait until he was older before he began investing. Like most people, he thought he had plenty of time, so he did not start investing $1,200 a year until the age of thirty. He continued investing $1,200 a year for thirty-six years at the same interest rate of 12%. Without looking at the total, would you assume that after the end of the 45 years Simon would have more money than Alvin? It would seem only fair, because Simon contributed $43,200 while Alvin only contributed $12,000, right? You are right about the amount the two individuals invested, but wrong about how compound interest works and the net result.

At the end of the 45 year period, Alvin was able to invest less and still end up with $1,394,742. Alvin made more money than Simon because he had a ten year head start. Simon invested over three times more than Alvin and was still not able to catch up. The reward only goes to the one who takes advantage of time and starts investing early. If you learn nothing else from this book, remember the importance of investing at an early age. The sooner you start the better.

Age	Alvin's Investment		Simon's Investment	
20	$1,200	$1,344	$0	$0
21	$1,200	$2,849	$0	$0
22	$1,200	$4,535	$0	$0
23	$1,200	$6,423	$0	$0
24	$1,200	$8,538	$0	$0
25	$1,200	$10,907	$0	$0
26	$1,200	$13,560	$0	$0
27	$1,200	$16,531	$0	$0
28	$1,200	$19,858	$0	$0
29	$1,200	$23,585	$0	$0
30	$0	$26,416	$1,200	$1,344
31	$0	$29,586	$1,200	$2,849
32	$0	$33,136	$1,200	$4,535
33	$0	$37,112	$1,200	$6,423
34	$0	$41,566	$1,200	$8,538
35	$0	$46,554	$1,200	$10,907
36	$0	$52,140	$1,200	$13,560
37	$0	$58,397	$1,200	$16,531
38	$0	$65,404	$1,200	$19,858
39	$0	$73,253	$1,200	$23,585
40	$0	$82,043	$1,200	$27,760

41	$0	$91,889	$1,200	$32,435
42	$0	$102,915	$1,200	$37,671
43	$0	$115,265	$1,200	$43,536
44	$0	$129,097	$1,200	$50,104
45	$0	$144,588	$1,200	$57,460
46	$0	$161,939	$1,200	$65,700
47	$0	$181,372	$1,200	$74,928
48	$0	$203,136	$1,200	$85,263
49	$0	$227,513	$1,200	$96,838
50	$0	$254,814	$1,200	$109,803
51	$0	$285,392	$1,200	$124,323
52	$0	$319,639	$1,200	$140,586
53	$0	$357,996	$1,200	$158,801
54	$0	$400,955	$1,200	$179,201
55	$0	$449,070	$1,200	$202,049
56	$0	$502,958	$1,200	$227,639
57	$0	$563,313	$1,200	$256,299
58	$0	$630,910	$1,200	$288,399
59	$0	$706,620	$1,200	$324,351
60	$0	$791,414	$1,200	$364,617
61	$0	$886,384	$1,200	$409,715
62	$0	$992,750	$1,200	$460,225
63	$0	$1,111,880	$1,200	$516,796
64	$0	$1,245,305	$1,200	$580,156
65	$0	$1,394,742	$1,200	$651,118

Someone may say, "I don't have $1,200 a year to invest." For now, don't focus on the amount you have to start with. The most important principle to learn is just to develop the habit of investing. Even if it is no more than $15 dollars a week, just start the habit of saving now. Over time, as you began to earn more money, increase your contributions. Remember: always pay yourself first.

Purchasing Items with Cash Versus Credit Card

In society today, it is normal for Americans to use debt (e.g. loans, credit cards, etc.) as a means for purchasing both big and small items. We are so programmed to charge everything to our credit card. "Charge It!" seems to be the popular statement among Americans. The average household has more than $10,000 in credit card debt. That equates to a household living two years above their means. In other words, it could take two years for most families to pay off this chunk of debt providing they don't charge another cent on their credit cards.

We are taught to use credit cards as a means of balancing our budget when we overspend. The truth of the matter is that our ancestors were wiser because they saved and purchased with cash. Whatever happened to using delayed gratification systems like layaway? Growing up, my mother would always use layaway to purchase items she did not have the cash to pay for at that moment. It is an old system that has started to come back around. I know some of you reading this book may be too young to remember this system so let me explain to you how it worked. When parents needed to go shopping for school supplies, they gathered all the items into their basket then took the supplies to the layaway department. The cashier rang the items up, my parent's paid a small sum of money on the total, and then the items were packed into boxes and stored in the back of the store. The items remained in storage until the remaining balance was paid. This policy required 10 – 20 percent cash down with the promise of paying off the balance within so many months.

Each week my mother paid cash on the layaway until she finally had enough to pay off the remaining balance. I love the concept of paying for the item before enjoying it instead of enjoying it and then paying for it later. Nine out of ten times, the final price for instant pleasure is usually greater than we think.

Opening a Savings Account

I initially struggled about whether to include this topic in the book or eliminate it altogether. There is a wealth of information to choose from and I wanted to only write about the topics that would be the most beneficial to the reader right now, so I deleted this section during the initial editing process. That was until a few months later when I read an astonishing article from CBS MoneyWatch.com that stated that children between the ages of 12 and 15 with a savings account in their own name are six times more likely to attend college than those without an account. The article referenced that the children who had ownership of their bank account and made their own deposits and withdrawals, expected to go to college in the future. The amount that each child had in their account was irrelevant as the average balance was around $400. Possessing an

> ***...children between the ages of 12 and 15 with a savings account...are six times more likely to attend college...***

account was the most important factor because the children started making responsible decisions that will have a long-term affect on their lives.

Opening a Checking Account

At some point down the road, once a child has proven himself to be financially responsible (e.g. keeping track of spending and bank balances), it may be beneficial for them to open a checking account in their own name. A checking account will allow them to use a debit card and to write checks from the account. The following example provides proof why I think it's helpful for children to have a checking account.

Now that my brother is in college, sending him money is a breeze. Instead of mailing him a check to buy books and so forth, I simply transfer the money directly into his account from my computer. This system works well for us because the bank we use does not have a branch at the school he is attending. If I mailed him a check, he would have to either mail the check off to be deposited in the bank (which could takes days), or wait until the next time he traveled back home (which would probably not be for several weeks). Plus, I like the fact that if an emergency ever comes up, I can send him money at the click of a button from my home.

The Debit Card is King

Most people like using a credit card because they feel they have more protection against unauthorized transactions. That is simply not true. You have the same protection with a debit card as you do with a credit card. It has been over six years since I have used or even owned a credit card. Once I found the path to wealth, I knew credit would not take me there. I use my debit card for every transaction that requires a credit card. My life has not changed one bit. I can do all of the same things with a debit card as I could when I had a credit card.

If you notice an unauthorized transaction on your account, contact your bank immediately to let them know about the error in your transaction history. They will require you to fill out the necessary paperwork in order to dispute the charge. Some banks have time limits for reporting unauthorized transactions, so it's a good idea to check your account a minimum of once a week.

Stay Away From Credit Cards

I am often bombarded with credit card offers in the mail. While shredding the offers, I am always reminded of the old folktale story about The Scorpion and The Frog. I am not sure who the author of the story is as I originally heard it from one of my CD collections. It depicts a classic example of how you cannot put your trust in things that are meant to harm you.

The Scorpion and the Frog

The story is about a scorpion asking a frog to carry him across a river. At first the frog refuses to do it because he is afraid of being stung. The scorpion reassures him that if he stung the frog, they would both drown. The frog agrees to the request. Nevertheless, in the middle of the river, the scorpion stings the frog, dooming them both. Before they sink, the frog asks the scorpion about his betrayal. The scorpion explains, "It's my nature; I'm a scorpion."

The story of the scorpion and the frog reminds me of my experience when I owned credit cards. No matter what the proclaimed benefits of needing to own one were, at the end of the day, debt is still debt. I remember signing up for my first credit card in college. When I received it, I made a promise to myself to only use it for emergencies. The funny thing is I don't remember ever having to use my credit card for an actual emergency. I can remember using my card to purchase a lot of items that I did not need. I have had around 15 credit cards in an eight to ten year period.

Over the years, I became a pro at surfing the balances on my cards. As soon as one card was maxed out, I would apply for another credit card with a higher line of credit from a different company. Once I was approved, I would transfer the balance of my maxed out cards to the new card. Once I maxed out my cards again, I repeated the cycle all over again. The debt continued to grow over the years. I deceived my own mind into thinking that I needed to build a high credit score through racking up charges on my cards to the maximum limit. Plus, the possession of a credit card was cool. I felt like a responsible adult simply because I paid all of my bills on time. My reasoning was that debt proved how responsible I was with money. Sadly, it was only an illusion. I found out that the exact opposite is true.

Quaneshala's Credit Card Saga

After I graduated from college and started my new job, I decided to get my first and only credit card. My thoughts were that I was on my way to building a high credit score. Each month I charged everything to my credit card. Having a credit card made me feel secure. I faithfully paid off the entire balance at the end of each month. I said, "I have finally arrived." I was confident that my credit score would rise to the top.

Years later, I married my fiancé, Adrian. During our engagement, Adrian helped me face the real truth about credit cards. He revealed to me that he had not used a credit card in over two years at that time. Adrian did not want us to begin our marriage with the bondage and deceit of credit cards. When I heard those words, I felt devastated. I argued the point that I could not live without my credit card, plus it only had a $1,000 limit. I wanted my future husband to understand how safe I felt with a credit card in my possession in case of an emergency. He then looked directly at me and asked a profound question. He said, "What's the difference between having $1,000 in cash set aside for an emergency as opposed to owning a credit card with a $1,000 limit?" There was no difference. Still, I felt better using my credit card on the basis of the new trend. Spending cash did not appear to be a normal practice anymore. The use of the credit card afforded me a delay in payment. Adrian won that argument when he announced that he would give me a $1,000 if I got rid of my credit card!

What's the difference between having $1,000 in cash set aside for an emergency as opposed to owning a credit card with a $1,000 limit?

We've had our debates over the use of credit cards, but I have acquiesced to his way of living and I'm glad about it. I have not used a credit card in over four years. It's hard to believe how quickly I became dependent on credit. The credit card's promise of security is an empty promise. I spent money on stuff I did not need just because I had a credit card. Those items would never have been purchased if I had been using cash at that time. It's quite sobering to now realize how much money I wasted just to be a part of a world that proudly promotes the false merits of credit cards.

You do not need a credit card to rent a car, reserve a hotel room, to travel, or even for an emergency. I declare to you that it is possible to do all of the above and more without a credit card. We have traveled to three different countries and within the United States. We have rented cars and reserved hotel rooms, and experienced several family emergencies. We were still able to handle each situation without borrowing money and without using a credit card. I can't explain the freedom that's involved in being able to buy the things needed and desired without any strings attached.

You do not need a credit card to rent a car, reserve a hotel room, to travel, or even for an emergency.

You might ask, "What about the rewards/points you can get by using a credit card?" Don't buy into the hype. By the time you rack up enough points to use, you could have just as easily saved up the cash to make the desired purchase. Besides, there are many advantages of using cash. Some of them include:

- Reduced stress
- Smarter purchases
- Cash only discounts
- Becoming a savvy spender
- Saving on fees in the long run
- Accumulating more money in the bank
- Developing patience to wait for a sale or discount

Cash will always be superior to credit. Credit cards have a "now and later" effect. You can indeed enjoy the product or the service NOW, but you will pay the price LATER. Will the high price be worth it when you do pay later? You decide. I do not regret my decision to desert my credit card habit. The application of these principles helped us to pay off our house within the first two years of our marriage. Now that's freedom!

> ***Do not go where the path may lead,***
> ***go instead where there is no path***
> ***and leave a trail. —***
> Ralph Waldo Emerson

Building Credit History

Most financial planners would lead you to believe that it is crucial that you start early applying for credit cards in order to build your credit score. They can give you 101 reasons on how credit can be used as a tool. They will tell you that having a high credit score will provide you with discounted rates when purchasing items such as airline tickets, car rentals, leasing apartments, buying insurance, or purchasing a home. You will walk away believing that it is virtually impossible to live a debt-free life.

Contrary to popular belief, living a debt-free life is different, but far from impossible. You don't have to build a credit history with credit cards in order to receive discounts from companies. If you follow our plan, you will be able to receive the same discounts others receive. For example, insurance companies give discounts to customers who pay their premiums in full every quarter. In addition, because there is so much competition between suppliers, you have the option to shop around for the best deal at any time.

Contrary to popular belief, living a debt-free life is different, but far from impossible.

Mortgage companies also give discounts to customers who make big down payments when applying for home loans. Again, by following our plan, you should have the money to pay cash for these purchases. Companies are mostly concerned about whether or not you have received a steady income over a given period of time. If you are living in an apartment, you can give them a copy of your rental history. Banks want to make sure that you are responsible enough to pay the loan back within the given period of time.

Credit History

Although you should not be concerned about building credit, you should be very concerned about the information contained on your credit report. There is a major difference between building credit and having a perfect credit history. The reason being is the only way to build credit is to constantly go into debt. It's a never-ending vicious cycle. On the other hand, maintaining a perfect credit report is easy. You will be only concerned about making sure you keep negative items off of your credit report.

Checking Your Credit Report

It is a good idea to check your credit report at least once a year. You can go to www.AnnualCreditReport.com and get a free copy of your credit report from the three major credit bureaus which are *Equifax, *Experian, and *TransUnion. You can check all three reports once a year. As a suggested practice, you may consider checking your report from one of the 3 credit bureaus every four months. In doing so, you may be able to catch discrepancies fairly quickly. Otherwise, by checking them all at once, you will have to wait until an entire year has passed from your last request before becoming eligible to view your credit reports for free again.

Visit the websites of Equifax, Experian, and TransUnion online to find their individual addresses.

How to Fix Discrepancies on Your Credit Report

Statistics show that 70 percent of credit reports contain errors. It's highly probable that you could be faced with the dilemma of having to correct your report at least once within your lifetime. Inaccurate data on your report could affect you in several different ways, such as having to pay a higher interest rate for a home loan or being denied a security clearance.

If you ever find yourself with an error on your credit report, don't worry, you have rights. The Fair Credit Reporting Act (FCRA), enforced by the Federal Trade Commission, promotes the accuracy, fairness, and privacy of information in the files of consumer reporting agencies. Below are the steps to correct inaccuracies on your credit report:

If you ever find yourself with an error on your credit report, don't worry, you have rights.

1. Identify the error and which credit reporting agency the error appears on
2. Send a certified letter explaining the discrepancy to each credit reporting agency where the error appears, with the inaccuracy highlighted on a copy of your credit report (send a separate letter for multiple discrepancies).
3. Send a certified letter to the creditor informing them that you are disputing the information they provided to the credit reporting agency
4. Keep an updated record of the date(s) the letter(s) were sent with a short description of the error.

The FCRA agency should notify you within 30 days with the findings of their investigation of your claim. If indeed the information was recorded incorrectly on your report, the agency will remove the inaccurate data from your file.

Credit Score

Lenders use your credit score, also known as your FICO (Fair Issac Company) score, to determine the level of risk they are taking when lending you money. The number gives lenders a picture of how responsible the individual applying for credit has been with paying back debts owed in the past. Most companies use the credit scores from one of the three credit bureaus (Equifax, Experian, and TransUnion). Scores are generated using the information each bureau keeps on file about you. Scores can range from 300 – 850. The higher the credit score,

Lenders use your credit score...to determine the level of risk they are taking when lending you money.

the lower the risk, and conversely, the lower the score, the higher the risk. High-risk candidates may be charged higher interest rates and fees.

Five Parts to Your FICO Credit Score

There are five parts that make up your FICO credit score. Below is a list of each part and how they affect you:

1. Payment History 35% - Includes late payments, bankruptcies, accounts in collection
2. Credit Availability 30% - Total outstanding debt
3. Length of Credit History 15% - How long accounts have been open
4. New Credit 10% - Number of recently opened accounts
5. Other Factors 10% - Type of accounts open

Please note that lenders understand that a high credit score does not necessarily mean you are guaranteed to be a good customer. Who knows what the future holds? You can just as easily lose your job as anyone else and become unable to make your payment. Lenders also use other information besides your credit score to assist them in make lending decisions. They have their own strategy to determine the level of risk they are willing to take.

...lenders understand that a high credit score does not necessarily mean you are guaranteed to be a good customer.

Don't Play the Game

Take notice of the fact that the only way to maintain a high credit score is to constantly go into debt. I don't know about you, but I am not going to stay in debt (bondage) just to keep a high credit score. I choose not to play The FICO Credit Score debt game. I decided to create my own game and call it my Wealth Score. Look at the example below. How would you judge these categories?

- Cash on hand 10%.
- Cash in savings 15%.
- Paid-for real estate 25%
- Investments 40%.
- Other/Personal Possessions (i.e. antiques, jewelry, cars, boats) 5%.

In this example, if you had a million dollars worth of assets and no debt, your credit score would be zero, but your wealth score would be off the charts. Who would you rather be? A person with a high credit score and a massive debt load, or a person with a high wealth score and almost zero owing? If my guess is correct, I am sure you would rather be a person with copious wealth and zero debt. So, don't fall into the trap of thinking debt is a powerful tool. It is only a tool for those who do not know that there is a better way to handle your finances.

...don't fall into the trap of thinking debt is a powerful tool.

Terry and Francine Miller

Francine attended one of our Financial Straight Talk Workshops held in Starkville, Mississippi. At the event, one of the discussion topics was whether it was possible to buy a home without first establishing a credit history. She enthusiastically raised her hand to comment on the discussion. She agreed that indeed this scenario was possible because her husband Terry had done it years ago before they were married. The audience was spellbound by her statement. They could not believe that a resident from their community had faith enough to achieve such a great accomplishment. His story was so inspiring that I decided to include it in this book. After reading this story, I am sure you will be just as enthused as the audiences were on that day.

Faith to Believe the Impossible

As a teenager, Terry dreamed about someday owning his own home. He promised himself that no matter how long it would take, he would eventually become a homeowner. He felt as though this would be an amazing accomplishment if he could achieve it. Little did he know that his dream would come true sooner than he had imagined. After graduating from college, he accepted a job in his hometown. Later that year, he decided to apply for a mortgage loan. He did not have a prior credit history so the loan manager turned him down. In spite of the loan manager's decision, Terry continued to have faith that one day he would be a homeowner.

A couple of weeks passed and Terry received a call from the bank manager. The man was calling to inform Terry that after reevaluating his application, they (the bank), decided to approve him for the home loan. Years later, Terry met and married the woman of his dreams. They have now been living in the same house for over 30 years. I am happy to report that their house is paid in full and they are excitedly anticipating retirement within the next few years.

Seek an Alternate Solution

I accepted an IT position in Richardson, Texas after graduating from college. Before moving from Florida to Texas, I decided to purchase my first car. I visited a couple of car lots and decided to buy a new Toyota Corolla. The salesman at first insisted that I needed a co-signer because I had not established a credit history. I expressed that I did not have a co-signer, but I did have the letter that contained my job offer. After looking over the letter, he decided to approve me for the car loan.

Please realize that there is always an alternate solution to any problem. Keep in mind that I am not suggesting that you go into debt to purchase a new car. I am simply informing you that having a credit history is not always the determining factor of you reaching a desired financial outcome.

Please realize that there is always an alternate solution to any problem.

For the record, I recommend purchasing used cars with cash until you have had an opportunity to build wealth. My decision to buy a new car was made before realizing that new cars lose the majority of their value within the first five years. A better option for me would have been to purchase an inexpensive car for cash that I could have driven until I was able to save up for a nicer used car in the future.

> ***If someone is going down the wrong road,***
> ***he doesn't need motivation to speed him up.***
> ***What he needs is education to turn him around. —***
>
> Jim Rohn

Beware of Student Loans

If you are preparing for college or presently attending a post-secondary school, you are very well aware of how expensive tuition and fees can be. Most students end up taking out loans to cover most, if not all, of the cost. I was one of those graduates with over $26,000 in student loan debt. My wife, on the other hand, went to school for free. It took a lot of planning and hard work, but she did it.

Most students end up taking out loans to cover most, if not all, of the cost.

I was unaware of the negative effect on my credit rating by taking out student loans. I felt that it was "free" money. I thought to myself, "I can just pay the money back after I graduate and find a job." I used to sit around all day thinking about the big salary I would start off with once I graduated. My plan was to have all of my student loans paid off in one year. That goal didn't turn out the way I planned.

A Change in Plans

I moved to Texas after graduating college with my Masters Degree from Mississippi State University in December of 2001. If you can remember, this was 3 months after September 11, 2001 (9-11). Shortly after, the IT industry began to decline. People across the country were losing their jobs. There I was, a new graduate, with a major in the exact field where people were being laid off. Quaneshala even lost her IT position in Richardson, Texas after working for her company less than two years. My dream of "making it" in the big city was shattered. After a month, I finally was hired as an Assistant Manager by a well-known retail company that sold shoes. I was very grateful to have a job, but my salary was below my expectations. There was no way I would be able to pay back my student loans and survive off of my monthly income. I quickly realized that I needed an increase in pay if I wanted to make payments on my student loans. Several months later, I applied for and was accepted into the Alternative Certification Program with the Dallas Independent School District. The pay was a lot better, but far from my dream salary. That said, I have to admit, I am thankful for the learning experiences I gathered in the classroom. I do not think my life would have turned out the way it has had I not accepted the challenge of becoming a teacher. Also, accepting the position gave me the extra money to start repayment on my student loans.

So, how do you fit in this whole situation? The point of me telling you my story will hopefully convince you not to accept any student loan money without first recognizing the cost. According to the *Wall Street Journal*, the average student loan debt for college graduates in 2011 was $22,900. I don't want you to be like the many college graduates who are still paying off student loans from over ten years ago.

My goal is to give you several options you can use that could possibly keep you from taking out student loans.

You may be wondering how you will be able to cover the cost of college without taking out loans. If you are in a situation where you do not have the finances to cover your college education, don't worry. My goal is to give you several options you can use that could possibly keep you from taking out student loans. Check these out:

Scholarships – depending on how far away you are from graduating high school will determine how much time you have to prepare for college. For example, my wife enrolled in Florida Bright Futures Scholarship Program when she entered high school. Upon graduating high school, she met all the requirements which resulted in the payment of her tuition at Florida A&M University. So, maintain a high GPA and take the SAT/ACT multiple times to see if you can improve your score. Colleges are always looking for students who have excelled in academics. If you are already attending college, you may be able to find scholarships that are offered by different departments. I was able to get a scholarship for my participation in several plays.

Resident Assistant (RA) – Becoming a RA could greatly help you by paying for your housing. When I attended Mary Holmes College, I became a RA my first semester. This was literally not heard of as only second year students could apply. It was truly the favor of God that helped me obtain that position.

Find a part-time job (Work Study if you qualify) – It is very possible to work and save for tuition each semester. If necessary, take one class at a time. Working your way through school may take a little longer, but you will not have to worry about the bondage of debt after you graduate.

Attend a Junior College – There is nothing wrong with attending a junior college right after high school. The tuition and fees are much lower than senior colleges. This will allow you to take all of the basic classes at a discounted rate.

You can always transfer to a senior college at a later date. Check in advance with the senior college of your choice to make sure they will accept the credits you earned from attending the junior college of your choice.

State Schools – It is typically cheaper to attend a college within the state you live. You will be surprised at how much of a quality education you can receive at a school within your state. Please don't misunderstand me. I am not knocking attending prestigious schools. If you can afford to pay the tuition, by all means, go. Just don't buy into the belief that you have to rack up over $100,000 in debt in order to have a valuable education. It's not what school you go to, but what you learn. There are a number of people who borrow a massive amount of debt only to end up working at a job with coworkers who attended a less expensive school yet are making the same pay.

Sponsors – Encourage parents, relatives, and friends to donate to your cause. Encourage them to donate to your college fund instead of buying gifts for your birthday or other special occasions. You will be surprised at the number of people willing to give for a worthy cause.

...find some way to attend college without accumulating debt.

If you decide not to take any of these suggestions, it's okay. The most important thing is for you to find some way to attend college without accumulating debt. My purpose is to encourage you to think outside of the box instead of just accepting that you have to take out student loans in order to get a degree. We certainly promote higher education. Quaneshala and I both have our Masters

Degree. Plus, according to the United States Census Bureau, college graduates with their Bachelor's degree earn over $1 million dollars more in their lifetime than high school drop-outs (see Average Lifetime Earnings Chart). The bottom line is that there are so many opportunities out there if you are willing to take advantage of them. The road may not be easy, but what is life without a challenge? So, seize any opportunity that becomes available.

Average Lifetime Earnings Chart	
Education Level	**Average Lifetime Earnings**
Professional degree	$4.4 million
Doctoral degree	$3.4 million
Master's degree	$2.5 million
Bachelor's degree	$2.1 million
Associate's degree	$1.6 million
Some college	$1.5 million
High school graduate	$1.2 million
Non-high school graduate	$1 million

> ***If you think education is expensive, try ignorance.*** —
>
> Derek Bok

Living the Good Life

College students may also be tempted to take out student loans in order to fulfill their personal desires. Do not borrow money in order to live extravagantly! I have watched many of my college friends use student loans to fund their leisure activities. Items include, but are not limited to:

- Parties
- Gifts
- Spring break vacations
- Off-campus apartments
- Down payments on a car

You are at the beginning stage of becoming an adult. It is now time to learn how to be totally responsible for your actions. Remember, the choices you make today will either hurt you or help you tomorrow. Ten years from now, let it be said that you listened to and acted on wise counsel. Don't follow the crowd into financial bondage. Be a leader and set the example. You will be years ahead of the pack by doing so.

> ***It's not whether you get knocked down; it's whether you get up. —***
> Vince Lombardi

MOUNTAIN CLIMBERS

With all the recent turmoil in the economy, a lot of people have lost their jobs or have had a drastic reduction in their household income. If you were not prepared for these current events, you may have found yourself with too many expenses and not enough income at the end of the month. Once you start to miss payments, it will not be long before the friendly creditors that were so excited to lend you money when the chips were up, will start calling and making payment demands when the chips are down.

The Mountain Climbers section is for individuals who need help getting out of debt. If you are stuck in a rut and need help climbing out of a mountain of debt, this will be the section that will help turn your life around. This plan was designed to teach you a proven way of eliminating debt fast. Even people who at first thought they needed to file for bankruptcy have been successful in taking back control of their finances after using this system.

Bankruptcy is Usually Not The Answer

I can think of three reasons why bankruptcy is usually not the answer to solve your financial problems. The first reason is because certain types of debt like student loans, tax bills/liens, criminal penalties, and child support cannot be forgiven. The second reason is because a bankruptcy stays on your credit report for 7 years. This could affect things like your car insurance rate, security clearance, and perhaps getting a job. The last reason is because the individuals who file for bankruptcy are only fixing the symptom; they are not attacking their bad spending habits.

Quick fixes will not work.

In order to change, you have to focus on the real problem. You have to face the real reason of why you are in this financial predicament. You have to change your philosophy about how you spend money before you will be able to stop repeating this cycle of jumping in and out of debt.

Quick fixes will not work. Only developing the right mindset and applying these strategies I am about to teach you will work. These are the same strategies I used to free myself from the bondage of debt. What you are about to endeavor may not be easy. You will have to sacrifice short-term pleasures for the purpose of gaining long-term financial success. Nevertheless, if you take the time and necessary effort to utilize the strategies within this section, they will work for you.

Facing the Truth

If you are late on paying your bills, I would not be surprised if you are receiving calls from creditors every day asking for their money. Dealing with creditors or collection agencies can be a challenge. The most common response will be to likely ignore them. We know we owe the money, but it is embarrassing admitting that we do not have the means to pay it back. It seems to be programmed deep within our subconscious minds to initially run away from our problems instead of facing them head on. It has been said that, "To err is human." You can trace this human tendency all the way back to the Garden of Eden with Adam and Eve. If you have experienced this, I totally get it. It's hard to be transparent with others. It's especially hard to be transparent with people who already know about our faults.

It seems to be programmed deep within our subconscious minds to initially run away from our problems...

I believe that our human desire is not to let anyone down. When we are not able to pay our bills on time, it can make us feel worthless as a person. You must understand that not being

I believe that our human desire is not to let anyone down.

able to pay your bills does not make you worthless and does not make you any less of a person. I had to come to grips with this a long time ago. The truth is that you need to change your beliefs about debt. It's possible that maybe if you had not placed yourself in a vulnerable situation, things would not be the way they are. Once you adapt a better financial game plan, things will surely start to turn around for you.

Dealing with Debt Collectors

The best way to deal with debt collectors is to call them before they call you. Let them know what your situation is on a weekly/monthly basis. Let them know that they will not get paid on time and give them the reason why. Make them understand that you acknowledge that you owe the debt and you are more than willing to pay it when your situation changes. Make sure you keep a record of all conversations you have with them. Collect information such as the time, date, name of the representative you spoke with, and a summary of the conversation. After you do your part, hopefully the creditors will interact with you in a respectful manner. The law prohibits them from harassing you, but some will push the limits if you don't know your rights. If you find yourself in a situation where a creditor is rude and nasty to you, hang up the phone. When they call back, explain to them that you demand to be treated with respect and that you will not tolerate harassment. Be firm in telling them that you will only agree to communicate with them as long as they remain professional.

Knowing What's Important

It is important for you to be crystal clear in understanding that the situation you are in has nothing to do with your value as a person. You were created in God's image. In other words, you are incredibly valuable. Keep that in the back of your mind if you ever find yourself in a situation of having to talk to debt collectors. If you don't have this understanding of your personal value, some debt collectors may try to intimidate you and have you convinced that paying them is more important than feeding your family. That is simply ridiculous. I saw this tactic demonstrated first hand. My mother (a few years before she passed away), who was battling pancreatic cancer at the time, was so concerned about paying her creditors that she occasionally neglected taking care of the important things like food, clothing, shelter. It was hard enough watching her slowly die without worrying about her involvement in personal neglect. I am not saying that she should not have paid them; what I am saying is that certain debt collectors should have been closer to the bottom of the list of being paid. There is no reason you should starve your family in order to quiet the debt collectors. At times we helped my mom financially, but I wish my mom had been more concerned about her health and with taking care of her necessities rather than making sure her credit cards were paid.

You were created in God's image..

Know Your Rights

It is very important for us as consumers to know our rights in order to avoid being taken advantage of by collection agencies. Knowledge can be very powerful if applied correctly.

The Federal Trade Commission, the nation's consumer protection agency, enforces the Fair Debt Collection Practices Act (FDCPA). The FDCPA prohibits debt collectors from using abusive, unfair, or deceptive practices to collect from you. A debt collector is someone who regularly collects debts owed to others. This could include collection agencies, lawyers, or companies that buy and collect delinquent debts. Below are a few example questions that are answered on the Federal Trade Commission's website (www.ftc.gov) about the Act:

- What types of debts are covered?
- Can a debt collector contact me at any time or any place?
- How can I stop a debt collector from contacting me?
- Can a debt collector contact anyone else about my debt?
- What does the debt collector have to tell me about the debt?
- Can a debt collector keep contacting me if I don't think I owe any money?
- What practices are off limits for debt collectors?
- Can a debt collector garnish my bank account or wages?

Visit the Federal Trade Commission's website for more about the consumer's rights against debt collection and other credit-related issues.

> ***The great breakthrough in your life comes when you realize that you can learn anything you need to learn to accomplish any goal that you set for yourself. This means there are no limits on what you can be, have, or do. —***
>
> Brian Tracy

Getting Current

Make sure all of your accounts are current before focusing on getting out of debt. This is especially true with IRS or child support payments. If you are several months behind on any bills, work out a realistic payment plan with your creditors so that you can get up to date with them. Creditors are usually willing to listen to you if you don't run or hide from them. If you are not able to pay the minimums, pay something. Sending any amount shows them that you are putting forth an effort to try to make the payment. In the event you are not able to send them a payment, continue to call them once a week to keep them informed of your situation. After you are caught up on all of your payments, then and only then, should you begin the Mountain Climbers section.

Lowering Your Interest Rate

If you have credit cards with high interest rates, you may find it beneficial to call the credit card company and ask them to lower your interest rate. You may be able to negotiate a lower rate if your balances are low and you have been a client of theirs for a while. What have you got to lose? It does not hurt to ask. The worst thing they can say is no. If they turn you down, at least you will be able to say you tried.

Here is another useful tip that may be very beneficial to curbing your debt

> ***If the high interest rate credit card company refuses to lower your rate, it may be worth taking the time to shop around for another credit card with a lower interest rate.***

load. If the high interest rate credit card company refuses to lower your rate, it may be worth taking the time to shop around for another credit card with a lower interest rate. If you are able to find a lower interest credit card, transfer the balance of the high interest rate cards to the new credit card with the reduced interest rate. Make sure you use this tip with discretion.

Let me give you two suggestions to consider before deciding if it would be wise to transfer your high interest rate credit cards to a card with a lower rate. First, if you have small balances that can be paid off fairly quickly, it may not be worth your time using this strategy. Second, don't take out a home equity loan in order to pay off your credit cards even if you can get a lower interest rate on this type of loan. Some financial planners would suggest that this is a wise practice because the interest paid on the debt can be used as a tax-deduction. This is a bad idea. By doing so, you will be trading unsecure debt (credit cards) for secure debt (home equity loan). The reasoning behind my objection to this practice is this: if you default on your credit cards, they cannot take your house, but if you default on your home equity loan, the bank may foreclose on your house and take ownership of it. Keep all unsecure debt unsecured.

Keep all unsecure debt unsecured.

Closing Credit Card Accounts

In some cases I have seen where it may be wiser to keep your credit card accounts open until you have paid off the balance in full. If you try to close your account before then, you may be hit with a higher interest rate. So, for the time being just shred all of your credit cards so you will not be tempted to use them.

As soon as you are able to pay one off, immediately call and close the account.

You may be reasoning in your mind, "I want to keep the account open in case I need it." Let's face the facts. There is no reason in the world to keep the account open unless you are anticipating going back into debt. Leaving the account open creates the temptation of some day using that credit card again. You can be assured that if you leave it open, sooner or later, you are going to believe you need it. On the other hand, when you immediately close the account, you instantly remind your subconscious that you now live by a new set of standards.

Let Sleeping Dogs Lie

My mother use to always tell me to let sleeping dogs lie when she saw me about to wake up old troubles from my past. She was warning me to leave dead relationships in the past. If the person was not trying to contact me, I shouldn't try to contact them. She reminded me that it was hard enough removing them from my life the first time. It wouldn't make sense to bring them back into my life again.

In comparison, you should not contact old creditors who are not currently trying to collect a payment from you. If you have old and unsettled accounts on your credit report that you have not paid in years, don't worry about bringing them up to date just yet. You can clean up blemishes off of your credit report once you have freed up some of your income by first paying off some of your current debt. If possible, wait until you have paid off your current debt and have saved up a lump sum of money before calling to settle with old debt collectors.

An exception to the rule would be if you owed things such as back taxes or child support. As I mentioned in the GETTING CURRENT section, you should pay those types of debt now. Try to save up some money as quick as you can to pay them off. The last thing you need is the government coming after you.

> ***One of the tests of leadership is the ability to recognize a problem before it becomes an emergency.* —**
> Arnold H. Glasow

Waking Up Old Debt

When you are ready to call and negotiate a deal to settle your old debts, start by first calling the creditor to whom you owe the smallest amount. Once you have cleared up that one, work your way up to the next smallest debt. Continue the process until you have completely cleared all of your old debt. Remember this: don't try to settle all of your accounts at one time. This is especially true if you don't have enough money to pay them all at once.

Depending on the type of account and how long it has been in default, you may be able to settle with companies for a fraction of the original debt. It is possible that the current charges may be drastically different from the original amount due to added surcharges, interest, and miscellaneous fees. When making an offer, keep in mind that the collection agency more than likely bought your account for pennies on the dollar. Please make sure that you receive their offer in writing before you send them a payment. Once you receive the proper paperwork, then and only then should you send them a payment to settle the account. Only send money orders. Never send them a personal check and never give them access to your checking account. They will more than likely clean your account out and there is nothing you can do about it because you legitimately owe them the money. Once the account is paid off, keep a copy of your receipt among your records for the rest of your life. You will never know if another collection agency will try to come after you again for payment on a bill that has already been settled.

Thunderstorm Emergency Fund

Before you start tackling paying off your debt(s), your first assignment is to save up what I call a THUNDERSTORM EMERGENCY FUND. This fund is money set aside in a savings account that can be used when extreme, unexpected, or unavoidable situations arise. The reason why I chose the name thunderstorm is because of the uncontrollable events that could occur while you are focused on getting out of debt. You can rest assured that there are going to be heavy rains that come along and try to ruin your day. Since we know that they are going to happen, it is important to take the time to plan for them. The goal is to only use this money when a crisis arises. This money purposely set aside will help take some of the unnecessary stress off of your financial situation. This fund will also keep you from going deeper into debt (e.g. using a credit card or applying for a loan), in order to cover an unforeseen expense. Believe me, it makes a tremendous difference when you have planned and are prepared for life's sudden events. Please don't be naïve and unwise to think that you will be exempt from the inevitable storms of life. We, as human beings, will continue to face problems as long as we live.

Believe me, it makes a tremendous difference when you have planned and are prepared for life's sudden events.

I recommend saving 1 – 2% of your gross yearly income. For example, if you make $100,000 a year, your Thunderstorm Emergency Fund could be between 1 – 2,000 dollars. I came to realize, however, that everyone's situation is different. Some people may need to keep more money on hand than others. To keep things simple, just stay within the 1 – 2% range. As a rule of thumb, try to have this money saved up within a month. Sell something if you have to in order to raise the money. Taking longer than a month to save your Thunderstorm Emergency Fund could slow down your momentum of getting out of debt. You may become discouraged quicker if you have not begun to see results. Here are some ways to quickly save up for this important emergency fund:

- Yard sale
- Sell items on eBay
- Start a side business
- Work overtime

A Qualified Emergency

After you have saved up the money for your Thunderstorm Emergency Fund, don't get itchy fingers and feet, run out and spend it just as fast as you saved it. This money is to be protected, not spent on careless items. If you have a problem with spending, put some distance between you and the money. Make it hard for you to instantly get hold of the money. If it is in a savings account, don't get a debit card for the account. This will force you to go to the bank during operating hours in order to make a withdrawal. Hopefully by the time you wait for the bank to open, get in your car to drive there, and walk inside to take out the money, the spending impulse will have disappeared. Another strategy you may try is to freeze the money. If you get the urge to spend it, you will have to wait several hours for it to defrost in order to use it.

Don't worry about trying to make any interest off of the money. This money should not be invested. Therefore, do not put it in any account that will cause your funds to be tied up. It should be readily available in the event you need it. Keep it in a money market or regular savings account so you can gain access to it quickly when needed.

Here are some guidelines to follow after determining that it is necessary to use your Thunderstorm Emergency Fund. When a situation has been justified as a true emergency, it's imperative to only use the exact amount needed to cover the cost of the emergency. No more, no less. Here is an example. If you become sick and need to go to the doctor, but you don't have enough money to pay the doctor's bill or to get a prescription filled, this would be the perfect time to use a portion of your Thunderstorm Emergency Fund money to cover

When a situation has been justified as a true emergency, it's imperative to only use the exact amount needed...

the cost. Use common sense and wisdom, and withdraw only the amount needed for the expense. Don't feel that you have the right to wipe out the entire fund simply because you had a little hiccup with your finances. This is not the time to go and pick up those designer jeans that you've always wanted because they are now on sale. Continue to remind yourself that the account is set aside only for emergencies. As soon as the emergency is handled, immediately stop your Debt Elimination program (you will learn more about this later in this section), and restore your Thunderstorm Emergency Fund back to the amount you originally predetermined.

Saved From the Summer Heat

I can remember when I decided to cut up my credit cards and never use them again. It was the summer of 2005. What do you think happened within a few weeks? That's right; you guessed it. I had an emergency to come up. The air conditioner in my home needed repairing. If you live in Texas, you know that air conditioning is a necessity during the summer months. Had I not already had a Thunderstorm Emergency Fund in place, I would have been forced to rely on credit cards again. There is no way to know for sure how that would have affected my decision to become debt-free. I don't think I would be where I am now. That was the day I was truly tested. Would I step over the line I had drawn in the sand? Would I go back on my commitment? No! After all the worrying, come to find out I only needed to add Freon to the unit. This was the first of many events that tested my determination and strength to say, "No" to the bondage of debt.

> ***Deliver thyself as a roe from the hand of the hunter, and as a bird from the hand of the fowler.* —**
> Proverbs 6:5

The Real Lesson

I can tell you countless stories about some of the challenges I faced while delivering myself from the bondage of debt. I remember having to have four of my wisdom teeth removed. One of my wisdom teeth caused the tooth next to it to form a cavity. The surgery was going to cost about $1,600 to have all four teeth extracted. I was worried about how I was going to pay for the operation. All I could think about was how I could use that money to pay off a debt. I was so focused on not being distracted from my goal of becoming debt-free that I trusted God to work the situation out. God provided a way. In the end I only had to come up with around $600 dollars before the surgery. Here's the kicker. When the surgery was over, the doctor told me that he only removed three of the four wisdom teeth. The doctor informed me that some slight complications may have occurred later in my life had he removed the fourth one. It's been over five years since I had that oral surgery and my teeth are just fine. I know this was God's way of saving me money because I received a $150 refund out of the initial $600 fee. A problem that I initially thought would cost me over $1,600 only cost me $450.

There is an important moral lesson to be learned from the

God will... supply all of our needs according to His riches in glory.

above testimony. Although I was very excited to receive a huge discount on my dentist surgery, there was more than dollars to gain from this story. The major lesson I learned was that God will [indeed] supply all of our needs according to His riches in glory. The key is to just believe.

Debt Elimination Strategies

Getting out of debt can seem hard and overwhelming. Most people agree that it seems to take only seconds to get into debt, but years to get out of it. I am about to show you four debt elimination strategies that most financial planners commonly use for eliminating debt. Although I will teach you four debt elimination strategies, I suggest that you use only three out of the four. The fourth debt elimination strategy should only be used as an exception to the rule. I will explain later how to determine whether or not you meet the criterion to use this exception.

...it takes only seconds to get into debt, but years to get out of it.

The four debt elimination strategies are **DEBT SNOWBALL, DEBT SNOWFLAKE, DEBT CALVING,** and **DEBT AVALANCHE**. My personal favorite is the Debt Snowball. I learned this debt elimination strategy from Dave Ramsey, a man I respect and admire as a mentor. He teaches this strategy in his book, *The Total Money Makeover*. This is also the strategy I am suggesting for your primary use to eliminate debt. Debt Snowflake and Debt Calving are great add-ons you can use to meet your financial goals much quicker. Debt Avalanche is the strategy I would only use as an exception to the rule. Some financial advisers promote this strategy based on the fact that you will save money mathematically by using it. They are correct concerning the mathematical part. The only problem with that reasoning is that obtaining financial freedom has very little to do with *crunching the numbers* and has more to do with *transforming your mindset.*

We will use Debt Calving and Debt Snowflake as an extra add on tool (supplement). This is because the Debt Snowball method is a consistent method you will use every month to help you get out of debt super fast. You will not be able to use Debt Calving if you do not receive large chunks of money on a regular basis. Debt Snowflake is a little more consistent, but you will not be able to get out of debt fast by only skipping a lunch here and there.

Debt Snowball

Debt Snowball is when you rate/order your debts from smallest to largest, regardless of the interest rate (see Debt Snowball Payoff Chart on next page). Then pay as much money as possible on the smallest debt while paying the minimum on the rest. When the smallest debt is eliminated, apply the same payment strategy plus the minimum to the next smallest debt, and so on. The Debt Snowball strategy is what Quaneshala and I used to accelerate our progress of getting out of debt. We used this method to eliminate over $90,000 dollars of debt in less than two years.

Debt Snowball Payoff Chart			
Payoff Order	**Debt**	**Interest Rate**	**Balance**
1	Car Loan	1.9%	$5,000
2	Credit Card	9.9%	$15,000
3	Student Loans	8.9%	$25,000

The Debt Snowball is truly the best strategy to use while getting out of debt...

The Debt Snowball is truly the best strategy to use while getting out of debt because it boosts your enthusiasm the fastest. Individuals will more likely stick with achieving their financial goals once they begin to experience a little success in eliminating debt. It's exhilarating to watch the debts, which you once thought were impossible to pay off, start to disappear. Like a locomotive engine, all it takes is a little traction to start moving forward. Once it has built up enough momentum, it becomes an unstoppable force. So, hang in there. Continue to make those first small, yet unnoticeable steps. Your hard work will soon pay off.

Debt Snowflake

Debt Snowflake is when you are able to save money on a regular day to day basis for the elimination of debts. This is a good supplemental strategy. One quick and easy way to implement this strategy is to start using coupons.

Coupons can help you save money when eating out, shopping at the grocery store, or on entertainment activities. Let's pretend that you've budgeted $60 a week for groceries. Coupons could perhaps save you $10 a week. That's $40 dollars of savings for the month that can be used to pay down your debts. There is no limit to the amount you can save. Get as creative as you can and come up with ways to save money.

One creative way I used Debt Snowflake was to take the cash, gift cards, and gift certificates I received on special occasions to pay off debt. If someone gave me a $20 gift card to Super Target, I would use it to buy groceries and then deduct that same amount of money from my allocated grocery fund. That left me with an extra $20 to use towards my debts. This total may seem small at first, but over time, it can really add up.

> ***Do not despise these small beginnings,***
> ***for the LORD rejoices to see the work begin.*** —
> Zechariah 4:10 NLT

Debt Calving

Debt Calving is when you take lump sums of money to pay off your debts. This money can come from any extra income whether expected or unexpected. By far, this is one of my favorite supplemental debt elimination strategies. It can be used to help accelerate the time it takes to get out of debt tremendously. I got the name Debt Calving from reading an article written by Liz Pulliam Weston, author of *The 10 Command-*

ments of Money, but I was using this strategy long before I realized what it was called.

When I first began my debt-freedom journey, I did not rely solely on my teaching salary for obtaining money. I believe that would have blocked all the other streams of income that came my way. Believing in other avenues of making money actually opened up multiple possibilities for me to increase my income. I could not have imagined all the sources of revenue that were made available to me simply because I kept my options open. I didn't become overwhelmed by wondering where the extra money was going to come from. My only responsibility was to be grateful for the new opportunities and to welcome them as they came my way.

During my years as a classroom teacher, I was presented with a number of opportunities that turned out to be lucrative sources of extra income. I signed up to work the after school tutoring program during the weekdays; I worked with the Saturday School tutoring program; and I worked for the Summer School program. All of this extra work increased my income. I received a minimum of $500 extra dollars a month. Since I was paid monthly, I used that money as my lump sum amount. I was also awarded a $10,000 student loan repayment grant for becoming a certified teacher. The receipt of that money really kicked my debt elimination program into gear. That was totally unexpected income. Thank you, Lord!

...look for ways to generate lump sums of money that can be used to apply to your debts.

My challenge to you is to look for ways to generate lump sums of money that can be used to apply to your debts. There are probably a number of opportunities already available to you of which you have not taken advantage. Take the time to explore all of the possibilities for creating additional income. We all know of one lump sum of money that a lot of people receive around the beginning of the year. It's called a tax refund. Use it wisely.

Here is an important piece of advice that I desire to share with you. I am constantly asked, "If a large sum of money comes my way, may I spend some of it for personal pleasure?" My immediate response is, "How fast do you want to be debt-free?" If you receive an expected or unexpected lump sum of money, apply all of it to your debt. I do understand that there are a few legitimate reasons for using some of the extra money (e.g. car repair, root canal, etc.). Remember, though, that this is not the time to take that vacation you've always dreamed about. Enjoy that vacation when you are totally debt-free. Please be mindful of the true fact that every dollar you waste can potentially postpone your goal of becoming financially free. On the other side of the coin, every dollar you spend wisely has the potential of bringing you closer to your financial goal. This is the perfect opportunity to show God that you can be an excellent steward of His money.

Debt Avalanche

Debt Avalanche is when you order your debts from the highest interest rate to the lowest (see Debt Avalanche Payoff Chart). The plan is to pay as much money as you can on the debt with the highest interest rate while paying the minimums on the rest. Once the debt with the highest interest rate is paid off, apply the same payment plus the minimum to the next debt with the highest interest rate. Continue this pattern until all debts have been paid off.

Debt Avalanche Payoff Chart			
Payoff Order	**Debt**	**Interest Rate**	**Balance**
1	Credit Card	9.9%	$15,000
2	Student Loans	8.9%	$25,000
3	Car Loan	1.9%	$5,000

Take a look at the Debt Avalanche Payoff Chart. You will notice that the payoff order is completely different than the Debt Snowball Payoff Chart. In this example, following the Debt Avalanche approach, you would take all of your extra money and apply it to paying off the credit card debt while making minimal payments on the student loans and on the car loan. Using this approach could potentially take years before you see your first victory in paying off a debt. After about a year of faithfully making extra payments to the debt with the highest interest rate, it's highly predictable that you will find yourself feeling bereft of any progress. You might give up on your goal of becoming debt-free because you're not seeing the expected results quick enough. Actually, the opposite is true. Mathematically, using this strategy will save you the most money because you will pay less in interest.

...using this strategy will save you the most money because you will pay less in interest.

This strategy may seem like the best way to start your Debt Elimination if you are only focusing totally on the numbers. Although I have mentioned this strategy, I do not recommend or encourage you to follow it because becoming financially free is 80% behavior changes and 20% knowledge. I am only sharing it with you as a point of reference. Again, I personally recommend using the Debt Snowball method because I know it works. In order to successfully stick with any task, you have to have gradual success and celebrations along the way. You need those little victories to remind you to stay focused on your ultimate goal of financial freedom. Waiting for years before being able to celebrate the pay off of a bill will be very discouraging.

There is, however, one exception to this rule. The only time I would ever recommend using the Debt Avalanche strategy is when you have debts that are close to the same balance with different interest rates (see Debt Avalanche Payoff Exception Chart). In some instances, even if the balances are small and close together, regardless of what strategy you used – Debt Snowball or Debt Avalanche – you may still end up paying the debts off within the same time frame.

Debt Avalanche Payoff Exception Chart			
Payoff Order	**Debt**	**Interest Rate**	**Balance**
1	Credit Card	29%	$2,229
2	Car Loan	10%	$1,783
3	Student Loans	2%	$2,019

The Freedom Date

Your freedom date is the day you anticipate becoming financially debt-free (with the exception of your house). Knowing your freedom date will give you a sense of power. You now have a reason to keep fighting for the life you deserve. It will also provide you with a sense of hope and encouragement when times get tough and when your strength to keep fighting is low. Don't spend time thinking about how much debt you owe. I remember thinking that it seemed as if it was taking forever for me to pay off my debts. Whenever I lapsed into the mood of feeling powerless, I would quickly snap out of it by remembering that with God's help, all things are possible. I reminded myself that this too, (being in debt), shall pass. Concentrate all of your thoughts on how you will feel once that day has arrived. Let your financal freedom date strengthen you despite challenges you may face. Make achieving your goal a special event. Think of a way to radically celebrate your victory of finally breaking the chains of financial bondage. When this day finally comes to pass, it will, without doubt, be one of your greatest moments of triumph.

> ***Let your financial freedom date strengthen you despite challenges you may face.***

Once you make up in your mind and set a freedom date, spend every day working towards achieving it. Who knows? By doing so, you may even end up achieving your goal sooner than originally planned! On the other hand, don't be concerned about not meeting your goal in your specified time frame. If you don't achieve your financial goal at the set time, set a new date. In spite of any failed attempts, keep reaching for your goal. You will be better off arriving at your freedom date at a later time than to not reach it at all. In other words, don't panic if you have to extend your freedom date to accommodate unforeseen events. The important thing is to decide on a date.

Your chances of realizing any goal drastically increase simply by setting a goal. Zig Ziglar always says, "If you aim at nothing, you will hit it every time."

I remember it like it was yesterday. I had set June 2007 as my freedom date to have all of my debts paid off (not including my house). I use to always fantasize about how it would feel to send in my last payment for my student loan debt. This was the highest debt on my Debt Snowball list. I must admit that I missed my original deadline by two months. I stopped paying off debt for several months in order to save and pay cash for my wedding expenses. Even though, I had to wait an additional two months, I was able to make my last student loan payment before my 30th birthday. Talk about a birthday to remember. This was a major milestone for me in more ways than one. I can laugh now at the memory of how I once believed that I would be making payments on debt for the rest of my life. You must make getting out of debt a top priority in your life. Otherwise, you will never be able to fathom the idea of what it feels like to be totally debt-free and to be able to pay cash for items instead of using credit.

Energy Flows Where Attention Goes

It is important to focus on increasing your income and on lowering your expenses while getting out of debt. Quaneshala and I have used this principle repeatedly throughout our marriage. Take note of the technique we used to pay off our house early. We set an initial goal to have our house paid off in three years. We had been married only six months when we set about accomplishing this objective. We believed this to be a fairly easy goal to accomplish if we lived off of one income. We were confident that we did not want to spend the next twenty-five years paying off our house by making only regular payments.

I printed out a spreadsheet... and taped it to our bedroom mirror.

I printed out a spreadsheet with the balance we owed on the house and taped it to our bedroom mirror. At the end of each month, we tracked our progress and prayed for continual blessings on our finances. All extra money we received was paid on the house loan. It was exciting to watch the balance drop lower and lower every month. A year into our plan found us a third of the way from our goal. We were making tremendous progress, yet I was dissatisfied with the results. I remember staying up all night thinking of a way to double our contributions in half the time. God helped me figure out a solution after much prayer and meditation. I challenged Quaneshala to agree with me on a plan the Lord gave me to pay off the remaining balance of $60,000 dollars within a six month period. We cut out all of our unnecessary spending and used any extra money (e.g. bonuses, pay increase) on debt. If you have read this far into the book, you already know we met our goal. That's the power of focus.

It was exciting to watch the balance drop lower and lower every month.

What You Look For, You Find

In the beginning of our marriage, Quaneshala and I got up on Saturday mornings to take a six mile walk in the neighborhood. We really enjoyed this time together because it gave us a chance to talk and to review our goals as a couple. During our walks, I never really took the time to look on the ground because I was focused on our conversation. One day, while walking our usual path, she found a penny on the sidewalk. I remember wishing that I had found the money instead of her. I know it was only a penny, but my wife has a way of rubbing it in my face when she finds things. She bragged about finding that penny for the remainder of our walk. I was ready for the walk to be over due to her good-humored boasting session. I believe that's why we get along so well as both of us have a great sense of humor.

We continued our morning stroll and she found some more money on the ground. I was beginning to get a little jealous by now. I began paying more attention to the ground. I was a little disappointed about not finding any money on our walk that day. I made a promise to pay more attention to the ground while walking with her in the future.

The following Saturday I also found money on the ground. I fully believe that the only reason I found it is because I was looking for it. Since that time, I can't remember when we didn't find money on the ground. One particular Saturday we found over $5 during our walk. Finding money happens so regularly now that we have turned it into a little game. We try to see who can find the most money during our walks. Somehow Quaneshala always wins because she finds more money than I ever do, but that's okay. I'm just grateful to end up with extra money at the end of our walking journey.

Stop All Retirement Contributions

While your focus is on getting out of debt, stop contributing to your retirement. I know you are probably saying to yourself,

"But my company matches my retirement contributions up to a certain percentage." That's great, but for now your main priority should be to get out of debt. If you follow the steps in order, there will be plenty of time to focus on investing. Otherwise, you may end up spreading your resources (income) too thin by focusing on too many goals at once (For example getting out of debt, investing for retirement, saving for the children's college, etc.). There is real power in focusing all of your resources on one goal at a time. If you still do not agree with me, just keep reading. This concept will make more sense as we delve deeper into this subject. You will soon begin to understand my reasoning behind stopping all retirement contributions and using the extra money on rapidly getting out of debt as your first priority. Remember, becoming debt-free is all about following the right strategy. Paying off debt first will put you in a perfect position to be able to invest more money later if you so desire.

There is real power in focusing all of your resources on one goal at a time.

Evaluate the Risk

In the summer of 2004, years before our marriage, I had a conversation with Quaneshala over the telephone. I remember explaining to her my grand master plan of investing substantially in my retirement account while maintaining a certain level of debt. I tried to explain to her my theory behind investing extra money each month into my retirement fund while making minimal payments on all my debts. She then told me that it would be wiser to pay off my debts instead of saving for retirement. She carefully explained that if I had a total of $10,000 in my retirement and $10,000 in debt, basically I did not have any money. I thought I had everything under control. My logic behind this theory was that by the time I was old enough to retire, I would surely be a millionaire. I thought that I could easily use a portion of my retirement money to pay off all of my debts. I was convinced that this was a smart plan because I had learned it from the smartest broke people I knew at that time.

A year later I finally realized the risk I was taking by investing into my retirement before paying off my debts. There is a very present danger that most of us don't take into account when making important financial decisions. Any time you borrow money, there is a risk associated with it. The higher the amount you borrow, the greater the risk attached to it. After evaluating the enormous risk I was taking by not paying off my debts, I decided to change my philosophy concerning the way I managed my finances. I stopped all of my retirement contributions and used that money to pay off my debt and it paid off in the long run.

Any time you borrow money, there is a risk associated with it.

Encountering Extreme Circumstances

Let's fast forward two years. I am so glad I made the decision to get out of debt when I did. Had I not made that decision, I don't think I would have been prepared for what was getting ready to happen in my life.

In January 2007, Quaneshala's oldest brother was murdered. Two months later, she received a job offer as a Business Analyst in Plano, Texas. I flew to Orlando and drove her back to Texas. In June, we were married. In one more month, I anticipated being able to send in my last student loan payment. Things were going great and I was on cloud nine. I never expected things to take a turn for the worse. On July 17, I received a call from my mother that my oldest brother had been murdered. I felt devastated. We hurriedly packed a bag and drove to Mississippi the next day. The news of my brother's death made becoming debt-free unimportant. All I could think about was being there for my family, financially, emotionally, mentally, physically, and spiritually. We attended the funeral then drove back to Texas. When we arrived home, the air conditioner went out. I wondered, "Lord, what else could go wrong?" As you know from reading about this last disaster earlier in this book, we ended up having to replace the entire air conditioning unit.

Lord, what else could go wrong?

After talking with Quaneshala, we decided it would be best to wait until August to pay the remainder of my student loan off on my birthday, which is what we did. We had an amazing evening. We enjoyed dinner at the Dallas Reunion Tower with a 360 degree view of the city to celebrate. During this same month, I was promoted from a classroom teacher to an Instructional Technology Specialist with the Dallas Independent School District. This was extremely good news, but with this blessing also came a higher level of responsibility. I had to manage around 50 teachers in 42 schools within the district.

In November, my mother became ill. The Doctors ran a series of tests, but they could not determine why she was in so much pain. In January 2008, my mother was diagnosed with pancreatic cancer. The doctor wanted to operate immediately. He told us that she had a 50/50 chance of making it through the surgery. On the day of the surgery, I lead a prayer with my mother, my wife, and several of my mother's friends in the hospital. I could feel the power of God in that room. I believe, through that prayer, God gave my mother an additional 20 months to live.

The Melting Pot

Many stressful events happened during our first year of marriage. We had no idea that God was preparing us for higher heights. I sincerely believe that my wife and I have a great calling on our lives. That's why it was important for us to make getting out of debt our top priority.

No one knows what the future holds. Most people believe that we only have to trust in God and everything will work out. While I agree 100% with this theory, I would like to go one step further however, by saying that God also wants to be able to trust us. How can He trust in us, you ask? God's desire is to trust us to be good stewards of the money He allows to flow through our hands. I'm glad I decided to get out of debt when I did. If I had decided differently, things would have turned out differently. I would have missed out on so many blessings and would have been unable to bless others. I have discovered that God's main reason for blessing us is so that we can be a blessing to others in the natural realm as well as in the spiritual realm.

God's desire is to trust us to be good stewards of the money He allows to flow though our hands.

If we provide only for our personal needs and desires, we are living very *small* lives.

> ***Every dollar you waste can potentially postpone your goal of becoming financially free. —***
> Quaneshala Johnson

Signs of Warning

God sends warnings to prepare us for the events that are about to happen. Read the story of Joseph and how God gave him the interpretation of Pharaoh's dream of seven years of great and plenty throughout all the land of Egypt followed by seven years of famine (Genesis 41:1-57). One choice Pharaoh could have made would have been to not listen to God's warning and just waste the seven good years of plenty. That's one option, but not a good one. The sad reality is that most people live their lives in this manner. They expect times to always be plentiful by ignoring the fact that famine could be right around the corner. Then they want to curse God when the famine comes. We are called to be financially responsible. It is our duty to be responsible with our money through proper planning when times are plentiful. The right financial planning will not allow the times of famine to catch us without resources.

...most people... expect times to always be plentiful.

The Real Reason for Getting on Track

What if I had made getting out of debt less of a priority? Where would I be now if I had ignored my debt and continued investing into my retirement account? What would have been the outcome had I not made the decision to become debt-free at that particular time in my life?

Let's consider how things would have gone had I not taken the debt elimination approach. Remember at the beginning of this book I had told you I was $35,000 in debt. My retirement account had peaked to around $16,000 during the time I decided to concentrate on getting out of debt. Considering all of the events of 2007 that required extra money, pulling funds out of my retirement account would have knocked a large hole in my savings. It would also have been the worst time ever to remove money from my retirement account because of the recession. Everyone was experiencing a 40% – 60% loss in their investments. My original retirement account of $16,000 had dropped to around $7,000. That's not including the fees, taxes, and penalties I would have had to pay for taking out the money before retirement age. Let's say that I could have taken out the $7,000 without paying taxes. I would still have lost over 40% of my investment. What a disaster!

The Ultimate Test

The hardest thing I have faced to this date was the passing of my mother. She lost her almost two year battle against cancer in 2009. There are days when I still grieve her death. In the months before she passed, one of her friends called to inform me that my mom had taken a turn for the worse. Since I was living in Texas and she was in Moss Point, Mississippi, I was under the impression that she was doing fine. I later found out that Mom wasn't telling me certain things because she didn't want me to worry. Quaneshala and I were enjoying a two week celebration at the time due to the fact that we had recently paid off our house during the month of July. When my mom's friend called me, she informed me that my mom was losing a lot of weight and her sickness was seriously affecting her. She was slowly getting weaker by the day. We cut our trip short and headed for Mississippi. Quaneshala and I met my mom at Walmart. She was shopping with one of her friends. When I saw her, my heart broke. The cancer had definitely taken its toll. I made an excuse to step around the corner outside the store. I didn't want her to see me cry.

I was able to take a leave of absence for almost three months after my mom passed away. I took this time off without worrying about losing my job with the added blessing of being debt-free. We almost made the decision at one point to move back to Mississippi for the sake of my brother. All of our miscellaneous bills in Texas (e.g. water, electric, phone) could easily be paid online. I didn't want to make a hasty or drastic decision, so I used the time I had off to bond with my youngest brother and to meditate on what actions I needed to take concerning his future. Freedom from debt afforded me the gift of showering my total attention on my brother without outside distractions. He was in his last year of high school. I made sure that his focus remained on graduating from high school. I took care of the other responsibilities that

Freedom from debt afforded me the gift of showering my total attention on my brother...

came with our mother's death.

Time off work also provided me with sufficient time to grieve. I had a lot of emotions to deal with. Deep within I felt that God was taking everything from me that meant the most to me. I had lost my older brother two years prior and now my mother was gone. This was a hard blow. I cannot fully express the wonderful relationship I had with my mother. We talked every day and, to me, she was my best friend.

The silver lining is that God placed Quaneshala in my life at the exact moment I needed her. She was with me when my mom died. She has been with me through thick and thin. We have shared all our failures as well as our successes together. I believe everything happens for a reason even if we don't understand the reason at the time we are experiencing the hardship.

A Turn of Events

If you are working your Debt Elimination plan and you become aware that a life changing event is about to occur, stop paying off debt and immediately start saving up cash. Some examples of life changing events include:

- Newborn baby or another addition to the family
- Loss of job
- Sickness
- Marriage
- Family emergency

After the event has passed and you are certain that everything is back to normal, continue your Debt Elimination plan. Take all of the money saved and apply it to your debts the same as before the event happened.

The Worst Can Happen

Mike recently lost his job and was working as a temp for a computer company. He called me and asked me if he should continue his Debt Elimination plan while working as a temp. I suggested that he stop his plan and save up any extra cash in the event he does not find a permanent job after his temporary job ends. I informed him that he could use the money saved to restart his Debt Elimination plan once he found a new job and finished his probationary period.

Less than three months later, Mike was able to find a new job. A few short weeks afterward, while making the transition and adjusting to his new job, he was in a major car accident. His car was totaled. It is amazing that he walked away with only bruises and scratches. After all the smoke cleared, he found out that he would be free and clear of his car loan, but without a car. The insurance company only gave him enough money to pay off the original car loan amount.

The insurance company only gave him enough money to pay off the original car loan amount.

It's a good thing Mike had taken our advice by stopping his Debt Elimination plan to start saving up cash for a rainy day. He was not worried because he had saved enough money to buy another car. Instead of being stressed out about the situation, Mike remained in good spirits while his body healed from the crash.

In addition to the inexpensive car he purchased with cash, Mike had enough savings to pay for several other unexpected expenses incurred by the accident. I'm sure that if Mike had not been changing jobs, he would have been okay using his Thunderstorm Emergency Fund to carry him until he was able to get back on his feet. Mike, though, was already in the process of learning how to live more financially responsible with his new income. Those extra savings helped to cushion the blow of his unforeseen mishaps without setting him further into debt.

> ***You were born to win, but to be a winner, you must plan to win, prepare to win, and expect to win. —***
>
> Zig Ziglar

TREND SETTERS

This section is catered toward individuals that have little to zero debt. The majority of a trendsetter's debt is owed on his/her house. Quaneshala is an example of this. Before she and I married, she could have written a check to pay off her credit card debt in a second. She only carried a balance because she had bought into the world's way of managing money.

If you fall into this category of having a small amount of debt that you could pay off in a heartbeat, this section is for you. You may have only kept your credit cards open because you bought into the propaganda of keeping them open helps you maintain a high credit score. Regardless of the reason, let it be a thing of the past. Stop listening to the advice of financial counselors who are just as broke as you are, but have the audacity to instruct you on how to be financially prudent. It's time to discover a higher road to financial freedom. The information in this section will teach you the importance of saving for a Hurricane Emergency Fund; investing for retirement; having complete coverage (e.g. car insurance, identity theft insurance, Will); saving for the children's college education; and paying off the house early. Here, in this section, you will begin establishing a system of wealth building – incredible wealth.

Stop listening to the advice of financial counselors who are just as broke as you are...

A Storm I Will Never Forget

I grew up in Moss Point, a small town located on the coast of Mississippi. Annually, the month of May was the month when conversations turned to the upcoming hurricane season. I worried each year whether or not this would be the year of the "big one." The generation before me always told stories about the horrors of Hurricane Camille which passed through in 1969 and about Hurricane Frederic which passed through in 1979. I was not born during Hurricane Camille, and I was too young to remember Hurricane Frederic. Yet, I still took each hurricane season very seriously. My oldest brother and I became accustomed to helping my mother prepare for potential hurricanes. Our preparation consisted of boarding up the windows, tying down the lawn furniture, and shopping for food and supplies in the event of a loss of power and water.

Over the years, we received several warnings of a hurricane heading in our direction only to have it later change course and go in a different direction. Secretly, I wished that the hurricane would stay on course and come through our area, but every year they turned away from us. Please be careful what you ask or wish for. A storm did finally find us and it turned out to be the worst storm of my life.

1985 was the year I experienced a major hurricane. Hurricane Elena was headed our way and the reports were not good. Local media encouraged everyone to evacuate the area. The other neighborhood children were excited, too, because this was our chance to experience what the older generation had already lived through. My mother, however, decided to avoid the storm. She drove us to her home town of Kosciusko, Mississippi, to stay with family until the storm passed over. I was both disappointed and relieved. Obviously I didn't really know what I wanted.

While in Kosciusko, Mississippi, for a few days, we heard

over the radio that the storm had changed course and was moving in the opposite direction. This news excited everyone and we packed up the car and headed back to Moss Point, Mississippi. On the way back home, we heard that Hurricane Elena had changed her course again. She was now headed in our direction. We were too close to home to turn around. We had no choice but to ride it out at home.

We all slept in one room during the wrath of Hurricane Elena. I heard the strange noises that were made by the strong winds yet I still fell sound asleep. I felt safe and secure with my mother sleeping next to me. The next morning we were amazed by all of the damage the storm had caused. Although I wanted to experience a hurricane, I did not give enough consideration to its resulting havoc. How could the elements of wind and rain bring about such devastation? We were without running water and electricity for days. Schools were cancelled for several weeks. I didn't think life would ever get back to normal.

Hurricane Emergency Fund

I'm sure you have been faced with situations that did not take a lot of financial resources to resolve. Some happenings have the power of surprise behind them and can turn your life upside down. Realizing the necessity of an emergency fund, I coined the phrase, Hurricane Emergency Fund. It has been designed to provide a financial buffer between you and the storms of life that will try to come in and cause financial havoc.

A hurricane emergency fund is when you have six months worth of savings in the bank.

A hurricane emergency fund is when you have six months worth of savings in the bank. Six months generally is enough time for life to readjust itself and return to normal. It's important for you to have that cushion. When my mother passed, it was nice not having to worry about how I was going to pay my bills because I had that hurricane emergency fund in place. It also made grieving the loss of my mother much easier.

I decided to share my hurricane experience with you because it is a perfect example of how the hurricanes of life can show up at your door. If you live long enough, it is highly likely that you will face a sudden, unexpected, perhaps tragic, situation that may require some of your financial resources. Although some financial hurricanes are not as bad as others, it is still important to have a six month Hurricane Emergency Fund in place.

A Hurricane Emergency Fund will give you peace of mind in the midst of your problems. It was years before I actually lived through a hurricane, but I'm grateful that my mother kept us prepared for the worst. A lack of planning would have landed my family in some serious trouble. We could have placed an unnecessary burden on the rest of our family due to our irresponsibility. Our mother knew that we lived in an area susceptible to hurricanes. She knew it was her responsibility to stay prepared for the hurricane season to hopefully minimize the effects of potential disaster.

The time to plan is now, not after the storm has passed.

The time to plan is now, not after the storm has passed. It is imperative that you take action today to build a financial wall that will keep the high winds of a hurricane from blowing you away. If you can do better, you should do better. You owe it to your family, your community, and to the world around you to better position yourself financially. Try earnestly to be an example for others to follow.

Is a Hurricane Emergency Fund Enough?

You may be wondering whether six months of income stashed away in your savings is enough to cover any hurricane you may go through. I don't think there is a set amount of money that can be considered enough. The sole purpose of these specific instructions is to teach you the importance of having in your possession a fully funded savings account. Over time, as you continue to build wealth, the amount of money in your account will increase. The main issue at this point is to simply set a savings goal and to work toward achieving that goal.

There may come a day when you will need help from other people. Just don't let the need for that assistance be due to your carelessness of not planning ahead. Outside aid becomes necessary when our problems are too large for us to handle alone. We do need each other. You too, should be prepared to go to the rescue of other people. Serious problems occur when you are only a taker and never a giver. That is not balanced living.

Serious problems occur when you are only a taker and never a giver.

Prepare for Retirement

After saving a fully funded Hurricane Emergency Fund, you are now ready to start preparing for retirement. I recently read an article about a survey of 401K plans which revealed that Asian employees contribute more than White, Black, and Hispanic employees. The study also revealed that Blacks and Hispanics are highly likely to tap into their retirement accounts more frequently than White and Asian employees.

- Asian employees contributed 9.4%
- White employees contributed 7.9%
- Hispanic employees contributed 6.3%
- Black employees contributed 6%

The United States of America, at the time of this writing, is over fifteen trillion dollars in debt! Yes, you read the amount correctly. The National Debt has continued to increase an average of 3.97 billion per day since September 2007. Our economy is in the shape it's in based on our bad habit of saying, "Yes" to more and more debt. We should be screaming a resounding "No!" to all debt.

> ***No man achieves great success who is unwilling to make personal sacrifices.*** —
> Napoleon Hill

Take Matters Into Your Own Hands

Answer the following questions. Are you willing to settle for a meager retirement? Do you want to be financially secure to enjoy your later years, or will you, for the rest of your life, barely get by on a substandard income? Years past, we expected Social Security to take care of us. Who knows now how much longer that system will be around? If Social Security is still around in 40 years, I seriously doubt that it will provide you with enough money to live a life of quality. Examine the lives of people who are currently dependent on social security checks. Are you envious of their financial status? If not, start saving for your future now.

You absolutely must start stashing away money for your retirement as soon as you can.

You absolutely must start stashing away money for your retirement as soon as you can. Saving for retirement should be fairly easy now that you are debt-free. It's a wonderful feeling to be debt-free, but the wealth building process is an even greater thrill. How much money would you like to accumulate for your retirement? What type of lifestyle do you envision for your golden years? Go ahead and fantasize about where you desire to live and what you desire to do upon retirement. This is your opportunity to dream big. Your answers to all questions concerning retirement will determine how much money you need to invest. The rule of thumb is to pick a number 10 times greater than your yearly expected retirement income. For example, if you have $1,000,000 saved in a Roth IRA, you can expect to draw a yearly income of $100,000. If your goal is to draw a $200,000 retirement check each year, then you will need to have $2,000,000 stashed away in a Roth IRA. The idea is to only spend the interest without touching the principal.

Your current stage in life will depict how much you can start off saving. Yearly investments can range anywhere from 10% - 25% of your gross yearly income. Saving 25% may be a little on the high end if you are in the beginning stages of building wealth and are at the same time taking care of a family. There are many factors to consider. Saving money for the down payment on a house, for instance, may hinder you from investing additional money into a retirement fund. The key, though, is to start investing as much as you can, as soon as you can.

Typically, single people without a lot of responsibilities or without extravagant lifestyles are usually able to invest more. This is also true for double income married couples who live off of one income. My wife and I have lived off of one income since we have been together. By harnessing the power of living this type of way, we have been able to radically grow our assets in a short period of time.

Find an investment advisor who will explain the ABC's of investing to you in an easy to understand language. Their primary goal is to make sure you are investing enough to reach your retirement goals. Make sure that you fully understand every investment to which you are contributing. Your investment advisor should be able to guide you with the knowledge of how to fund your Roth IRA, 401K, and ESA (if you have children). Stay away from purchasing single stocks and annuities unless you are a stockbroker and have a complete knowledge of this system.

Find an investment advisor who will explain the ABC's of investing to you in an easy to understand language...

Typically you should start investing in Roth IRAs first because they grow tax free. Investing in 401Ks or 403Bs will be the second best option if you work for a corporate or organizational institute. Make sure you are taking advantage of any retirement matching programs your company may offer. There is no sense in letting this free money go to waste. When you sit down with your investment advisor, he/she can determine which strategy will best help you acquire your ultimate financial goal(s). They should be able to give you a clear picture of how much of a monthly contribution you will have to make in order to reach your retirement objective. Please make sure you are investing in a well diversified portfolio.

Regardless of what stage of life you are at, consider investing a minimum of 10% of your annual gross income. The key is to just make a start. Don't worry if the amount is only a small one at first. It's important to begin developing the habit of investing, especially at an early age. Over time, as your income goes up, start drastically increasing your savings. Your investments should also go up as your income increases. Just remember to keep your expenses down. Contributing to investments will become easier and easier as you do it on a consistent basis. Watching your retirement fund grow is exciting.

The Power of Investing

Let's say your gross yearly income is $41,500. If you saved 10% for retirement, that would equal $4,150 you could use to invest each year. Each month, you could contribute $345.83 into your retirement account. If you invest this amount at 11% in a ROTH IRA for the next 35 years, you will end up with around $1,719,976. That's right. You will have over a million and a half dollars, tax free, in your retirement account. The best part is that you will have only contributed $145,249 out of your pocket. The $1,574,727 is from the interest gained from consistently investing over a long period of time. That sounds like a lot of money to me. How does it sound to you?

Let's take a look at more examples that show the power of investing. In Example 1, the person who started at age 20 was able to save over a million dollars more than his friends. The others were only able to save a fraction of what Person 1 saved because they had less time to invest. In Example 2, in order for Person 4 to end up with the same amount of money for retirement as Person 1, he has to invest $3,187 additional dollars a month. I don't know about you, but I would rather be as wise as Person 1 and start investing early instead of paying the price for waiting until it's almost too late.

Example 1

Investment Chart	Person #1	Person #2	Person #3	Person #4
Age	20	30	40	50
Starting Balance	$0	$0	$0	$0
Annual Rate of Return	11%	11%	11%	11%
Monthly Contributions	$100	$100	$100	$100
Number of Years Contributed	45	35	25	15
Retirement at Age 65				
Total Contributions	$54,000	$42,000	$30,000	$18,000
Total Interest	$1,454,543	$455,346	$129,058	$27,885
Future Value	$1,508,543	$497,346	$159,058	$45,885

Example 2

Investment Chart	Person #1	Person #2	Person #3	Person #4
Age Starting	20	30	40	50
Balance	$0	$0	$0	$0
Annual Rate of Return	11%	11%	11%	11%
Monthly Contributions	$100	$303	$948	$3,287
Number of Years Contributed	45	35	25	15
Retirement at Age 65				
Total Contributions	$54,000	$127,260	$284,400	$591,660
Total Interest	$1,454,543	$1,379,700	$1,223,471	$916,604
Future Value	$1,508,543	$1,506,960	$1,507,871	$1,508,264

It's Never Too Late

Looking at the examples above, you may be a little discouraged if you can relate to Person #4. Listen: don't beat yourself up about it. All you can do is be thankful that you are taking action now. It is never too late to start. Don't walk around wishing you had found out about and had taken heed of this information years ago. That's unproductive. The best thing you can do at this moment in time is start where you are. Focus on the changes you are still able to make. You do have time to leave some kind of legacy. Even if your legacy is just shining a light to help the younger generations avoid your financial mistakes, it will be a legacy worth leaving. It is our moral responsibility to teach our youth that sound financial decisions should begin while they are still young.

...if your legacy is just shining a light to help the younger generations avoid your financial mistakes, it will be a legacy worth leaving.

Celebrate Your New Financial Destiny

If you have made it this far with your new financial plan, now is the time to celebrate your accomplishment. You should be proud of the fact that you have taken control of your financial destiny. You must give yourself a chance to breathe from all of the hard work. You have accomplished so much. You had to make real sacrifices to pay off a mountain of debt. Since you have kept your expenses low and have consistently invested for retirement, you should have money left over to use for other goals.

In the past, I did not think it was important to take the time to acknowledge victories. I was not accustomed to having fun with money. My normal routine was to start a project, endure the pain of not quitting, and then finally accomplishing it. I spent much time and a lot of hard work accomplishing my goals. I never took the time to reward myself whenever each goal was achieved. My only satisfaction came from the knowledge of an accomplished objective. I repeated this cycle year after year. Hindsight now reveals my self-deprivation.

This "all work and no play" cycle, although it was of my

own making, made me resentful of my good stewardship. My financial agility didn't seem to be worth the effort. I was blessing everyone with nice gifts, but leaving myself unrewarded. I had always wanted to be a blessing to other people, yet I didn't feel blessed even when I was blessing others. It was strange. People were enjoying my money more than I was enjoying it.

Quaneshala taught me a better way. My marriage to her helped me become more balanced in this area. I came to realize that it was actually not a sin to enjoy the fruits of my own financial labor. I am now filled with great joy whenever I sow goodness into the lives of other people.

So, go ahead and find something that excites you and do it. We're talking about something within reason, of course. Women, if you desire it, go on and buy that outfit you saw in that store. Men, go ahead and buy that gadget that you have been wanting so badly, but decided to put it off in favor of heavier responsibilities. Plan your vacation. When you return home from your trip this time, however, you will not have credit card debt waiting for you. You are now able to pay for your vacation in cash! What a wonderful feeling! Your earlier financial sacrifices have paid for your vacation in full.

...go ahead and find something that excites you and do it.

Here is another interesting fact. You will probably be able to get a better deal by paying for your vacation and for other items in cash. I find it so amazing that the people with the cash to pay for items tend to spend less for them. The people without cash really can't afford the items they want, so they end up spending more money for their purchases by using credit.

Keep Celebrating

You have celebrated your recent victory for becoming debt-free. You have saved a Hurricane Emergency Fund. You have started an investment account. Great job! Now, for the rest of your life remember to acknowledge your small accomplishments as well as your major ones. Perhaps you can throw a victory party once a year so friends can help you celebrate your steadfastness in financial matters. You can even plan big celebrations on a 3-5 year basis. These time span celebrations will give you the energy and encouragement needed to continue living a lifestyle of financial freedom. All celebrations do not have to cost a lot of money. Save the extravagant celebrations for the accomplishments of your 5-10 year goals. The key is to take time to celebrate along the road of your financial journey. Celebrations will make your journey much sweeter.

> ***Celebrate what you want to see more of.* —**
> Tom Peters

Planning for Children

If you don't already have children, this may be the perfect time to start your family. Now that you are out of debt, you can focus more of your attention on important matters like starting a family. You don't necessarily have to be completely out of debt to begin your family, but it does help when your finances are in order.

Stay at Home Mother/Father

Today, a mother who stays at home with her children is more a rarity than the norm. Mothers are oftentimes forced to pick up the slack when fathers are absent from the home. When a marriage is intact, it usually requires two incomes just to survive. Now that you have a better financial plan, however, remaining at home to nourish your children is an option. Here is a way to test this plan of action. Practice living off of one income while still bringing in two. If you can successfully do this for a six month period, you are likely ready for the transition. Six months should be enough time to test the waters of one income living.

The job of stay-at-home mother/father can be very rewarding if you can adhere to a certain lifestyle.

On the other hand, if you cannot remain disciplined enough to keep from tapping into your second income, you may need to figure out more ways to decrease your spending. The job of a stay-at-home mother/father can be very rewarding if you can adhere to a certain lifestyle. Find out what matters most to you. Will you still be traveling to exotic locations around the globe every year, or will you, as the primary caregiver, practice financial wisdom in order to stay home and watch your children grow up?

Children's College Fund

Studies show that 50% of college graduates have student loan debt which averages around $10,000. You already know from my story that I had accumulated over $26,000 worth of debt by the time I graduated with my Master's degree. You are a

Trendsetter. This is the perfect time to plan for your children's college education. You can open up an Educational Savings Plan for each child. Sit down with an experienced investment advisor for assistance in choosing the right educational account that fits you.

If your children are on the verge of attending college, or if they are already attending one, don't feel bad if you are not able to pay for their tuition. My mother, in spite of her inability to pay for my tuition, was still an awesome mother. I didn't think any less of her simply because she was unable to fund my college education. My love for her would not have been any greater had she been financially able to pay for my college tuition. I'm certainly thankful for her help in other ways while I attended college (e.g. car, clothes, food, gas, etc).

Parents, please don't sacrifice your retirement for the sake of sending your children to college. That's not wise. Don't let guilt make your decisions for you. Funding your retirement should always be placed above funding your child's college education. Your future is what's important at this point. When your children are grown, married, and gone, it's unlikely that they are going to take care of you as they will have their own families. Trust me; they want you to plan your own future. You will be less of a burden on them later by taking care of yourself now. So, set yourself up first. Look back in the Future Stars section to get helpful advice on how to attend college without taking on any student loan debt.

> ***Funding your retirement should always be placed above funding your child's college education.***

Trade Up in Car

If you are tired of driving that old clunker, it may be time to trade it in for a new car. There are a lot of nice, affordable cars available. Don't forget, though, the advice mentioned in the Future Stars section. Cars lose their value quickly. The goal is not to go back into debt just to have a nicer ride. Save up the money and pay cash for a better car.

Paying Cash for a House

This is the most exciting section for me. I will never forget the morning we submitted our last house payment to the bank. We were so ecstatic. I felt a new level of freedom that words cannot explain. This accomplishment was definitely worth all of the difficult and disciplined sacrifices we made in order to make our home ours and ours alone. God definitely gets the glory.

I will never forget the morning we submitted our last house payment to the bank.

Whenever people hear about our miraculous story, they immediately want to know, "How did you guys do it?" Well, looking back, I can remember the times when frustration set in and I was tempted to stop working my Debt Elimination Plan. It was during those times of temptation when I remembered an amazing story.

I had read about a couple and their astonishing accomplishment. This young married couple saved $200,000 in a period of four years with a total annual income of $80,000. They lived in an upstairs garage apartment after they graduated from college because the rent was inexpensive. It's possible that most of their family and friends disapproved and felt that the couple was crazy for choosing such a lifestyle. This couple, however, ignored the criticism for an entire four years and focused only on their ultimate goal which was to purchase their first house with cash. They did not allow the opinions and the small thinking of others keep them from pursuing their dream.

Guess what? When the four years were up, they purchased a house for $150,000 and the wife used the other $50,000 to buy furniture. WOW! How fantastic is that? This ordinary couple had accomplished in four years the same thing that it takes most Americans to accomplish in thirty years. Their story in its entirety is featured in Dave Ramsey's book, *The Total Money Makeover*. I'm sure it will inspire you as it did me and I encourage you to read the book. So, during those years of anxiously working toward financial freedom, I kept this couple's story in mind. I believed that one day, I too would be completely debt-free. Their testimony gave me the hope I needed to fight another day.

Dreams of Owning a House

If you are in the market to buy a house and are not able to pay cash for it, save up a minimum of 20% of the house price for a down payment. This way you can avoid paying the Private Mortgage Insurance (PMI). Take out a 15 year loan. Banks usually offer lower interest rates for 15 year mortgages as opposed to 30 year mortgages. You can also take advantage of special programs that some banks offer to their customers. When I first bought my house, I was offered a special interest rate since I was a first time home buyer.

Can You Afford It?

When you are ready to start the loan process, don't be pressured into borrowing over your limit. Keep a loan amount in your head and determine that you will not go over that amount. You should stick to a monthly payment around 25% of your take home pay. Remember, after making the house payment, you still have to eat. Make sure you have enough money to live off of after the mortgage is paid. I have seen too many people get in over their heads. They associate the high mortgage approval as a blessing from the Lord and purchase homes at the maximum dollar amount available to them. They eventually end up losing their house and blame God for the loss. It wasn't God's fault. They were way out of their price range in the first place.

Paying Off Your House Early

If you already have a mortgage, now is the time to consider the benefits of paying off your house early. You don't have to refinance even if you're locked into a thirty year mortgage. Did you know that if you pay 1 extra payment a year, you can possibly knock off 7 years on a 30 year mortgage? Little steps like this can potentially save you tons of money. Take a look on the facing page at the House Payoff Table. Mortgage #1 has a loan amount of $100,000. If the loan is paid off in thirty years, the total interest paid at the end of thirty years will be $93,259. That's almost double the original cost of the house. An extra payment of $537 a month on your mortgage can save you $66,434 in interest payments. Ten years later you will have paid for your house in full.

If you are not able to double up on monthly payments, send in what you can. Look at Mortgage #2. This loan amount was $200,000. The owners sent in an extra amount each month equal to half of their regular mortgage payments. Just paying an extra half payment still saved them $82,228 in interest. They cut the years owed on their loan in half!

If you are intrigued by these examples, start making extra monthly payments on your mortgage today. Send in a separate check to your mortgage company with a note that reads, "Apply Extra Payment to Principal." You will soon discover that you are the proud owner of a "paid off" residence.

House Payoff Table	**Mortgage #1**	**Mortgage #2**
Loan Amount	$100,000	$200,000
Interest Rate	5%	5%
Number of Years to Pay Off House	30 yrs	30 yrs
Monthly Payments	$537	$1,074
Total Interest Paid at End of Loan	$93,259	$186,518
Extra Monthly Payments		
Amount	$537	$537
Number of Years to Pay Off House	9 yrs & 11 mo	14 yrs & 8 mo
Years Saved	**20 yrs & 1 mo**	**15 yrs & 4 mo**
Interest Paid	$26,825	$82,228
Interest Saved	**$66,434**	**$104,290**

The Tax Write Off

I'm amazed at the number of people I have spoken with who label a mortgage as *good debt* because of the tax write off. What they fail to understand is that debt is just that—DEBT! The risk does not go away simply because it appreciates in value. It is not your property until you own it! The best thing you can do is pay it off as soon as possible. Think about it. Does it make any sense at all to pay banks thousands and thousands of extra dollars for the purpose of saving a few pennies from the IRS? I don't think so.

Does it make any sense at all to pay banks thousands and thousands of extra dollars for the purpose of saving a few pennies from the IRS?

Most tax professionals persuade homeowners to keep their mortgage in order to receive a tax write off. I agree that the interest paid to the bank is considered a tax write off. I totally disagree about it being a write off worth keeping. If you are one of the many people struggling with the idea of paying your house off early in fear of losing the tax break, keep reading. Take a look at the Mortgage Tax Break Chart. On Example #1, the yearly interest payment to the bank is $10,000 from a loan amount of $200,000 at a 5% percent interest rate. Carefully examine the chart and you will see that the tax deduction from the IRS would only be around $2,500 using a 25% tax bracket from a taxable income of $90,000. Now ask yourself this question. "Am I willing to pay the bank $10,000 in interest payments in order to save $2,500 in tax deductions from the IRS?" I certainly hope not. It's no wonder the banks are getting richer by the second. We're making them rich, and in most cases, due to our lack of knowledge.

Mortgage Tax Break Chart	Example #1	Example #2
Loan Amount	$200,000	$500,000
Interest Rate	5%	10%
Interest Paid to Bank at End of Year	**$10,000**	**$50,000**
Taxable Income	$90,000	$250,000
Tax Bracket (Married Filing Jointly)	25%	33%
Tax Deduction from IRS	**2,500**	**$16,500**
Total Interest Paid to Bank	$10,000	$50,000
Money Saved from IRS	–$2,500	–$16,500
Total	$7,500	$33,500

> *Whatever the mind of man can conceive and believe, it can achieve.* —
> Napoleon Hill

Starting a Business

Starting a business can be hard work, but very exciting. Do you have a business idea that you have been contemplating? This is a great time to start a debt-free business. You should be aware by now of our stand on borrowing money to start a company. Don't buy into the hype that you have to go into debt to grow the company. Stay away from loans. Save the money you may need for startup costs. Do not jeopardize all of the hard work you put in to become debt-free.

When we started our company, The Heart of a Teacher, we used cash to cover all of our expenses. All of our debts (except for the house), were paid off at the time we began our business. We used the money that we no longer needed for debt to invest in our company. The freedom of using cash to grow our company has been most rewarding. We were able to keep a lot of the expenses down by being creative and by optimizing things we already possessed. I converted one of our bedrooms into an office. Most of our consultations are done over the telephone. If I need to meet with a client, we schedule a meeting with them at a public location like Starbucks or the public library. Regardless of the challenges you face, there are alternatives. Whatever the problem, there is always a solution. You may have to be a little creative in finding the answer, but there is always a way.

Make sure you invest your hard earned money wisely into your business.

Take this precaution: Make sure you invest your hard earned money wisely into your business. Stick to an industry of which you are well familiar. Don't fall into the trap of investing into something that "seems" like a good idea. So many people have lost enormous amounts of money because they listened to other's tales of supposedly amazing success. Study the market you are interested in. If you don't have the hours to invest in learning the ins and outs about the particular business you would like to pursue, it's a clear sign that you may be on the verge of making a big mistake. The future of your company depends on your whole-hearted attention. It is an absolute must that you first stop and think before partaking in any business endeavor.

Cash Opens the Door

Now that you have cash, you will find out that you can get unbelievable deals on items you buy. My wife and I are always trying to find a fascinating deal because we can pay with cash. It's kind of funny how people with money pay less for the same items than people without money pay for them. I was that person in times past who paid ridiculous prices for things I could not afford. Not so now.

Now that you have cash, you will find out that you can get unbelievable deals on items you buy.

Give Me A Deal

One of the first items we promised to purchase after we paid off our house was a new mattress. We shopped around at three stores. Our mission was to go to each store and buy from the one that had the best deal for the highest quality mattress. We probably laid on 15 beds in the first store we entered. I told the sales person that we were serious shoppers and that we were going to buy a mattress today! We told him to offer us his best deal for the mattress my wife and I liked the most. He gave us his best offer. We informed him that we would check out his competitors before deciding on a final purchase. We left and went to two other stores and repeated that same process.

We found that store number one had the mattress we liked the most, but store number three offered a comparably cheaper mattress with free delivery. We would have been content with the exceptional deal offered to us by store number three, yet our hearts were still leaning toward the mattress at store number one. We went back to store number one to see if he could beat the deal offered to us by store number three.

When we arrived back at store number one, we immediately looked for the sales person who worked with us earlier that day. We told him of our findings and asked if he could beat the price offered by store number three. Throughout our conversation he kept running back to his computer to get special permission in order to drop the price. He offered to beat his competitor's price after fifteen minutes of wasted time. He gave us the run around about free delivery. He proudly told us that everyone has to pay the cost of delivery, but I thought to myself, "I am not everyone."

We spent another five minutes listening to what he could and could not do, and so on and so on. I was beginning to experience frustration and fatigue. I was ready to buy a mattress and go home. I firmly stated to the sales person that it had been a long day and that my wife and I were ready to buy. "Are you able to make this deal or not? If not, we will go buy the mattress from your competitor. It's that simple!" You should have seen the expression on his face. I guess they didn't teach him how to handle frustrated customers in Sales 101. I caught him off guard with my demands because I was tired and ready to leave. His only response was, "Yes, sir, you can have free delivery."

The story gets better. While we were standing in line preparing to buy the mattress, the couple in front of us was purchasing the exact same mattress. It was the last mattress of its kind in stock so ours had to be placed on backorder. The only thing we could think about at that moment was, "MORE DEALS!" The sales rep did not want to lose our business by any means, so he included an $89 mattress protector free of charge. We walked away with a discount on the mattress, free delivery, and a free mattress protector. How? We had cash.

The mattress was not as important to us as was scoring a great deal. Our use of cash gave us the power to walk away from one store with the purpose of negotiating at another store. This ability to walk away is a very powerful weapon that can be utilized by the consumer when making purchases. Sales representatives will not negotiate with you when you make them cognizant of your desperation regardless of the item's price. The salesman knew that we were serious about taking our business somewhere else.

Wait. I don't want to give you false impressions. This technique does not always work for us. There were times when we really did have to walk away because the sales rep would not budge on the price. What usually happens is that after waiting for a little while longer, we find the item somewhere on sale anyway. Sometimes we have found something even better than what we had originally planned to purchase. Here are some simple techniques you can use when shopping for bargains:

- Don't seem overly excited
- Act as if owning the item does not matter
- Always ask if that is their lowest price
- Let them know that you are comparing prices with their competitors.

> ***Expect the best, plan for the worst, and prepare to be surprised.* —**
> Denis Waitley

Complete Coverage

Having the right coverage is part of a complete financial package. It's important to make sure you have a shield of protection guarding the assets you have accumulated up over time. Here is the truth about insurance: *it's better to have it and not need it than to need it and not have it.* Below are some of my personal recommended coverage plans.

A Will

Once you start accumulating wealth, wisdom dictates that you draw up a Will. It's unfair to force upon your family the responsibility of dividing your assets. They do not know how you want your estate distributed and the last thing you want to do is cause division within your family as they fight over who gets what. Please don't give the state the power to divide your assets. It's even possible for the state to end up with a portion of your estate without an established Will. Family fights and outside involvement can be avoided by having this important document in place.

Family fights and outside involvement can be avoided by having this important document in place.

People tend to shrink away from the duty of filling out a Will because they erroneously think that doing so will somehow force them into an early grave. Filling out a Will has nothing to do with your death date. That's silly thinking. A Will is not for you; it's for the one who is left behind sorting out your assets. A Will proves to the person left to handle your estate just how much you care about him/her. It is cruel to make someone else responsible for something that only you can truly handle. If you do die earlier than anticipated, everyone will be glad you left instructions concerning the handling of your affairs. Your family will have a difficult enough time dealing with your death. Ease their burden. Take care of your business while you're still alive and well.

Automotive Insurance

There are a lot of companies that can offer you a competitive price on automotive insurance. If you do not own renters or homeowners insurance, it's best to shop around for deals. If you do own a house, check with your insurer to see if they offer multiple policy discounts. Usually you can save a lot of money this way. You may also find it beneficial to switch to a higher deductible (e.g. $1,000 versus $500). If you own an inexpensive car (say under $1,000), check to see how much you can save by switching to liability with uninsured motorist. Now that you have a fully funded Hurricane Emergency Fund, you can buy another inexpensive car in the event your current car is totaled.

Renters Insurance

Renters insurance is good to have if you are currently living in an apartment. In the event of a fire, your possessions will be covered. It is unlikely that your landlord's insurance company will pay for your personal possessions in the event of a disaster. If you are in college and living in a dorm, but are still a part of your parent's household, you may be covered under their policy. However, if you are living in an apartment and not in a dorm, you will probably need your own renter's policy. Policies vary, so discuss with your insurer the insurance policy that may fit your specific situation.

Homeowner Insurance

It goes without saying that it is a must for you to have homeowners insurance on your home. Why waste the time trying to pay it off if only to lose, possibly your most expensive asset, to some catastrophic event? Most policies cover against fire, lightning, wind, explosion, theft, vandalism, and a host of other specific causes of damage or loss. Banks will require you to carry a homeowner's policy before securing a loan. Because the bank has a financial interest in your home, they are smart enough to make sure that their investment is protected if a loss occurs. If you are responsible for paying your own homeowners insurance, make sure you don't let your policy lapse. A lapse in insurance coverage on a home that carries a mortgage can lead to lender-placed insurance, often at ridiculous rates. It's possible that rates could triple the cost of a regular homeowner's insurance policy. Any losses that occur during the lapse of insurance would not be covered.

Why waste the time trying to pay it off if only to lose, possibly your most expensive asset, to some catastrophic event?

Term Life Insurance

Term life insurance provides coverage at a fixed rate of payments for a limited period of time. Term insurance is the least expensive way to purchase a substantial death benefit on a coverage amount per premium dollar basis over a specific period of time. Investing in term life insurance is the perfect insurance to have until you are self-insured (i.e. a calculated amount of money set aside to compensate for the potential future unforeseen loss). Open a term life policy that is 8 – 12 times your gross annual income. If you earn $50,000 a year, you should have between $400,000 - $600,000 dollars in coverage. The number of years will depend on how long it will take you to become self-insured. You will also need to take into consideration the age of your children. You may need a longer term of coverage if you have younger children. If having children are in your future plans, consider a higher time frame like 25 – 30 years of coverage. That way the policy will not expire until after they are in their adult years. One of your main concerns should be assuring that your spouse is not left with the burden of finding a way to support the family. In case of a catastrophic event, it's important to make sure the surviving spouse is able to pay for necessities like babysitters, clothes, shelter, and college.

Identity Theft Insurance

I read a story in the news about a company that threw away its employee's paperwork. The paperwork was not shredded; it was thrown into an outside trash bin. This paperwork contained confidential information (e.g. Social Security numbers, birthdays). Someone, thank God, noticed the information and reported it before the garbage was scheduled for pickup. This is a classic example of how carelessness can cause so many people to have their identity stolen through no fault of their own. According to the FBI, identity theft is

According to the FBI, identity theft is one of the fastest growing crimes in the United States.

one of the fastest growing crimes in the United States. Over 2 million people have had their identities compromised in a data breach since 2005. One in five families has been a victim. It has recently been discovered that babies are now the target of ID Theft. NBC's Jeff Rossen reported that thieves are stealing the Social Security numbers of babies and raking up massive debt without discovery until many years later.

Victims of Identity theft spend countless hours trying to undo the damage to their credit. This can be a nightmare if you are trying to straighten it out by yourself. Due to this alarming problem, I recommend investing in Identity Theft insurance. Pick a company that offers prevention services, full-managed victim recovery, and reimbursement assistance for the expenses you incur. If you ever become a victim of identity theft, you are not going to want to spend countless hours trying to restore your identity. Let the identity protection company spend the time clearing up your record for you. They have trained professionals that handle fraud cases on a regular basis and most likely will complete it faster than if you were handling this matter yourself.

...I recommend investing in Identity Theft insurance.

Picking the Right Team

You should have a team of advisors to rely on for important information. Surround yourself with the right network of people. Make a list of all the business people you know along with their contact information and a detailed description of their expertise. You never know when you will need their services. Don't worry if your current list is short. It will grow as you meet new people with different skills. I am always adding to my list of contacts. Whenever someone performs a service for me, I keep their information handy in case I need their service again. A trustworthy team of professionals and skilled laborers can be a very nice addition to your life. You will find examples below of people you may consider adding to your team.

- FINANCIAL ACCOUNTABILITY PARTNERS: These people are supposed to help you reach your overall financial goals. Their purpose is to make sure your financial goals are balanced and within reach. They should serve as your accountability partner(s). They can be a friend, family member, or financial company (e.g. *Financial Counseling from The Heart of a Teacher*) you trust. Make sure they are either successful at managing their own finances, currently working on their own financial goals, or have a proven track record of helping other individuals achieve similar goals. They should consistently check to make sure you are meeting your daily, weekly, monthly, and yearly goals. Someone to encourage you along the way will help ensure your success in reaching your financial target.
- CERTIFIED PUBLIC ACCOUNTANT: Some people perhaps wonder why an accountant is needed when they are accustomed to preparing their own taxes. An accountant is necessary because the tax laws are constantly changing. You need professionals who are staying current with all the changes. They will make sure you are taking advantage of all the tax breaks. A CPA will see that your tax documentation is filed correctly to the IRS. A seasoned professional will be able to find savings that you may have possibly overlooked. You will be surprised at the

number of people who do not take advantage of crucial tax savings or who file their taxes incorrectly each year. A CPA who you know and trust is a major plus. You can pick up the telephone and call them anytime you have a tax related question.

- LAWYER: You never know when you will be in a situation that will require a lawyer. We had to seek out the opinions of several lawyers on how best to handle my mother's estate after her death. Lawyers specialize in various types of services. Some help with filing patents, creating a Will, filling out a power of attorney, etc. When you run across one of these professionals, take their information, and keep it on hand.
- CONTRACTOR: Quaneshala and I are always looking for contractors that can help us with routine maintenance around the house. The services we need are varied. We hire out for our sprinkler system, painting the house, repairing the garage door, shampooing the carpet, and plumbing just to name a few. When looking for the best deal from a contractor, always make sure they are licensed before letting them perform any work. Don't ever fall into the trap of taking "the easy way out" and choosing the least expensive, because you will end up spending more money for a real contractor to come fix what was supposed to already be fixed.

> ***Can two walk together, except they be agreed?*** ***—***
> Amos 3:3

STAYING TOGETHER

Money is considered to be the number #1 cause of marital problems that has led so many people to divorce. *Staying Together* was designed to teach engaged, newlywed, and married couples how to function as one unit with their finances. This program will help couples begin to make sound financial decisions together. Starting a new life with someone is challenging enough; money problems do not need to be added to the equation. Reading this section will enable you and your partner to join forces as one and will empower you to manage your money as a team.

Thinking About Marriage?

Marriage can be a touchy subject when one or both parties involved are faced with a mountain of debt. Quaneshala shared a story with me about a woman who was contemplating marriage. However, once this lady confided to her fiancé that she owed over $100,000 in student loan debt, he left her. Ouch!

Personally, I think it is perfectly fine to marry while in the middle of your Debt Elimination plan. Quaneshala and I married a few months before I became debt-free. I stopped my Debt Elimination plan after I proposed to her in order to save $4,000 in cash to pay for my portion of the wedding. By the way, make sure you look for ways to keep wedding expenses down. We did not spend a lot of money on our wedding because we knew we had other financial goals that were more important to us. Don't be persuaded by family and friends to overspend on your predetermined budget. Yes, you can have a very nice wedding at an affordable price. For example, instead of outsourcing decorations, see if you can do them yourself. We were very fortunate to have family pitch in and help with some of the wedding expenses. We requested that our guests give us gift cards instead of the usual wedding presents because I already had a fully furnished house we were moving into after the wedding.

When choosing a partner, make sure that you and your future spouse are in agreement about living a debt-free lifestyle.

...make sure that you and your future spouse are in agreement about living a debt-free lifestyle.

You can easily discern how your potential spouse is with money by watching his/her current spending habits. If overspending is a problem while he/she is single, those same bad habits will be brought into the marriage. Please heed this warning: Do not make any contributions toward paying off their debt until after the two of you are married. Anything can happen within the time period from your first meeting until the date of your wedding. I know couples who thought they were living with the person of their dreams. Further down the road they ended up marrying a completely different person. If the wedding is called off, you may never again see the money you gave to help pay the other person's bills. The best advice I can give to you is for you not to pretend, or act, like you are married while you are still single. Do not make any financial commitments before the "I do's" are said. There will be plenty of time to make financial decisions as a couple. Assistance in paying off each other's debts should only be done once the marriage has taken place, not a moment before.

"And Two Shall Become One"

It is important to carefully choose your life partner. The famous words "I do" are meant to last forever. Let's take a moment to consider what this statement means. This commitment signifies that everything he/she has belongs to you and vice versa. Whatever baggage one brings to the table, whether it is bad spending habits or a huge amount of debt, all of that now belongs to you. The debt may not officially be in your name, but since it has to be repaid, the total household income will be affected. You should fully understand every part of a person with whom you are about to connect. Don't think that the person is going to change simply because you have tied the knot.

Look at each other's credit report. Launch an investigation to see whether or not he/she pays bills on time. If the one that you think you are in love with runs up huge amounts of debt and fails to pay those bills on time, that's a red flag. It is not too personal to ask someone about their financial background before you marry. Please get over your fear of hurting the feelings of your potential partner by asking for this information. If a discussion of real issues offends them, you do not need to be with them. Anything that has the potential of affecting your future with the other person needs to be discussed. You cannot look at this type of discussion as a violation of trust. You must check the facts.

Anything that has the potential of affecting your future with the other person needs to be discussed.

Think of it this way. Most states require that you get a blood test before marriage. What if your fiancé or fiancée finds out during a routine physical that he or she has a terminal illness? Would you expect to be informed about their illness before the wedding? Of course you would! You have the right to know all of the facts before you make such a huge commitment. Honesty after marriage is useless and unfair. Trust me; you will not want to find out after the honeymoon is over, that your spouse has a closet full of skeletons. Deal with the problems now rather than later.

My primary goal is to make you aware of the risks that people sometimes take in the name of love.

Just because a problem does arise, doesn't remove the fact that you may love them. It's not my place to decide whether you should or should not marry that person—that's between the two of you. My primary goal is to make you aware of the risks that people sometimes take in the name of love. Keep your eyes wide open when making important life decisions.

Have you seen the movie, *A Walk to Remember*? This film was based on a true story. The characters, Landon and Jamie, overcame a difficult challenge. Landon fell in love with Jamie only to find out later that she was sick. Jamie's illness did not stop the couple from spending their remaining time together as Landon chose to be with Jamie in spite of her illness. Their love for one another outweighed the circumstance they faced.

There is Still Hope

Is there hope for your relationship if you are already married? The answer is YES! There is still hope. We provided counsel to a couple who had been married for ten years, but had not worked on their finances as a couple. In thirteen months they paid off over $27,000 worth of debt. It took ten years for this couple to reach their breaking point. They finally realized and admitted that they needed help. Once we formulated a plan that worked for them, transformation was easy.

It's not impossible for your spouse to change. You may, however, be in for years of hard work, sweat, and tears before the change happens. I am spending a lot of time in this area trying to help single people think before they impatiently jump into marriage. It's easier to start a relationship off right than to try to change your spouse and your situation after the wedding celebration is over.

Keep reading. I will address different ways throughout this chapter of how the two of you can make the same financial transformation made by the couple above.

Top Five

There were five qualifications that a woman had to meet before I would even consider her as my potential partner for life.

1. Faith
2. Boundaries
3. Children
4. Money Manager
5. College Degree

For starters, my future wife had to be of the same faith as I since I was determined not to be unequally yoked with an unbeliever. Along those same lines, my future wife needed to have a desire for ministry. I prayed and asked God to send me my Priscilla (Acts 18:26). I wanted my significant other to be passionate about investing into the spiritual lives of other people. The Holy Scriptures warn us that two people cannot walk together unless they are in agreement. My wife and I would have to agree on the same things in order to build a life together. Our dreams, our desires, and our expectations had to match. I came to the realization early on in my life that the person an individual marries will either add to (make you better), or subtract (make you worse), from that individual. Second, there had to be boundaries among our family and friends. I was determined to keep the in-laws in their proper place. All decisions made by my wife and I had to be based on what was best for our relationship, not based on outside influences. Third, the woman I married had to have a desire for children. I wanted to leave a legacy to my son or daughter. Fourth, my life partner also had to be a good steward over money. I plan to someday be a millionaire. That would be virtually impossible if she was not disciplined in the art of building wealth. Fifth, I wanted my wife to have a college degree among her possessions. My desire was to marry someone who had been exposed to higher education because self-development is very important to me.

Plan for Success

Notice that the first 4 out of the 5 qualifications on my list of marital needs are the primary reasons relationships end in divorce. I attended marriage seminars, workshops, and read relationship books years before I decided to look for a wife. I refused to wait until I was ready to get married before I spent time understanding the complexity of marriage.

In those earlier years of attending seminars and workshops, I watched couples disagree on what seemed to be trivial matters. The root of their problems usually stemmed from a lack of agreement concerning the handling of finances. I see this same pattern of disagreement year after year.

Some of the problems I have heard couples complain about are overspending by the other spouse; not being allowed to be involved in financial decisions; bullying tactics used toward their spouse in order to justify unsound financial decisions; or timidity because the other person is the breadwinner.

No matter the excuses, one spouse does not have more rights than the other. You have been called by God to be "One" with each other. Before my wife and I could say "I Do", the minister had us to repeat the wedding vows after him. Included in those vows was the truth that all of my worldly goods belong to her and all of her worldly goods belong to me.

No matter the excuses, one spouse does not have more rights than the other.

No person is always "up" all the time. We all have our down moments. I practice giving Quaneshala an equal voice in our relationship. I never want her to feel like she cannot express her opinion on anything in our marriage or in our household. When all of the decisions we make are soaked in prayer, those decisions come out alright. If the tables were turned and

Quaneshala was the sole provider, my hope and prayer is that she will give to me the same respect and honor that I give to her throughout the years. No man is an island unto himself. We all need each other.

The Enlightenment

I did not always manage money well. Remember my admission in the beginning of this book that I believed in error that I had to spend my entire paycheck in order to be financially successful? I was operating under the false illusion that I was enjoying life to the fullest, but in reality I was broke, sick, and desperate. I am amazed at how I held on so strongly to such a ridiculous philosophy. I have truly come a long way.

> ***...I had to spend my entire paycheck in order to be financially successful...***

When I first moved to Dallas in 2002, I met Quaneshala at a church that we both attended. She eventually lost her job, but remained in Dallas for another six months before moving back to Florida. We kept in touch with each other for several years. We were just friends at that time with no thought of ever becoming a couple. During those years we talked on the telephone for hours. We could go months without talking to each other, but whenever we resumed our telephone conversations, we picked up where we had left off from the previous one.

One of those conversations involved deciding which financial achievement was best to accomplish first—debt freedom or retirement stability. This conversation happened when I was over $30,000 in debt. My genius plan was to invest $6,000 a year into my retirement (I discussed this in the Mountain

Climbers section). She, of course, insisted that I pay my bills off first and then focus on saving for retirement. Quaneshala was already debt-free. She made the decision during our telephone conversation that night that she did not want to become romantically involved with someone who was entangled with debt. Yeah, the truth really does hurt.

She is the One

In November of 2006, Quaneshala came to Dallas to spend the Thanksgiving holiday with me. This trip was pre-planned to determine whether or not the two of us could build a life together. When she arrived, we talked about everything except finances. I was afraid to bring up the subject. I knew that she did not have any debt, but I knew nothing of her money saving techniques. Did she save money or did she spend money foolishly simply because she had no debt? During that Thanksgiving week, I found out that Quaneshala met four of my five qualifications for a wife. I knew she would be a perfect fit for me if I found out that she could manage money.

I will never forget those last moments we shared on our last day together. We had an hour left before it would be time for me to take her to the airport. I finally gathered the courage to ask her about her financial situation. She answered the question with the answer I needed to hear. Then I knew. I knew at that very moment that I wanted Quaneshala to be my wife. That special hour brought back to my memory a prayer that I had lifted up to God concerning my future wife. Since I had

I will never forget those last moments we shared on our last day together.

not been in a hurry to marry, I was always in a position to pray this prayer: "Lord, whenever you send my wife to me, please show her to me." It seemed as though, at that very moment, she appeared. It's a lot easier to remember that moment than it is to explain it. It was indeed miraculous! I proposed to Quaneshala a month later on Christmas day. We were married six months after my proposal. Outside of receiving Jesus Christ as my Savior, marrying Quaneshala was the best decision I've made in my life.

Blessings Delayed But Not Denied

God will sometimes withhold things that we are not yet mature enough to receive. We can miss out on God's promises if we despise correction and if we refuse to change. I'm certain that I missed out on many opportunities because of my refusal to grow. We must act when the season is right or we run the risk of postponing our blessings. I'm so glad that Quaneshala waited until I decided to change my attitude about money management before entering into a relationship with me. Our marriage is much stronger due to my decision to study the secrets of wealth. I dumped my debt before we became "One."

We must act when the season is right or we run the risk of postponing our blessings.

Why should Quaneshala sacrifice her life's savings, accomplishments, and goals by tying herself to someone unequal to her financial prowess? One of her sisters always warned her against marrying someone buried in debt. Her sister obviously knew that debt could cause a lot of unnecessary stress in the marriage. I am so happy to admit that we do not have fights about money. I think our biggest arguments derive from where the temperature on the thermostat should be set! Quaneshala enjoys heat and I enjoy the cold, so the problems don't go away. They are just easier to deal with when your finances are in order.

One Can Chase a Thousand and Two Can Chase Ten Thousand

In an earlier section of this book, I wrote about my plans to pay off $35,000 worth of debt in less than two years. What I did not mention in the story is that I also had a plan to pay off my house in seven years if I remained a single man. That plan meant that I would have paid off everything except the house by the summer of 2007, and would have paid off the house by summer of 2014. Things did not go according to that financial plan because I met the woman of my dreams and married her.

January 2008, after being married for six months, Quaneshala and I decided to pay off the house in three years by paying an additional $30,000 each year on our mortgage. This strategy did not put a big strain on our income. We were still able to travel and enjoy ourselves with the money we had saved. One year later, however, we decided that we did not want to wait another two years to pay off our house. I came up with a strategy using the same principles I teach in this book to rapidly pay off our house in six months. The plan that we both agreed on was to drastically cut out all waste. We scrutinized every area of our budget. If we did not need it, we did not spend money on it. We did without. During those six months, for some reason, I developed car fever. I really wanted to take some of the money we were putting on the house and use it to buy a used car. I had to finally ask myself one simple question. "Adrian, would you rather own another car or would you rather own your house?" Well, I guess you know what I chose.

This is a powerful testimony. It clearly demonstrates how extraordinary things can happen when couples become laser focused on one single objective. Dreams can be accomplished rapidly. Quaneshala and I took two years to accomplish a task that would have taken me seven years to accomplish alone. I was saved from five extra years of debt enslavement!

Freedom from debt has transformed our lives in so many ways. Our outlook on life has completely changed. Our thoughts and even our conversations, showcase this beautiful change in our lives. Life is so remarkable now. It is truly a feeling you will have to experience in order to understand. If you follow the secrets in this book, you can enjoy the same freedom we live every day. I am just an ordinary person. I used to believe that I would be in bondage to debt my entire lifetime. Not anymore! You too, can have an extraordinary life.

Freedom from debt has transformed our lives in so many ways.

Freedom from debt is only the beginning. There is another level of freedom to obtain once you have mastered this level. There is so much more of life out there for you to explore. There is a realm of possibilities waiting for you. Don't be like most people and remain on this level. If they only knew that the ultimate fulfillment comes on the next level. Continue your journey. That's what this book is all about. It was written to awaken you to your purpose in life. You will really begin to live when you reach "*The 4th Level of Financial Freedom.*"

Being in Agreement

We do not counsel couples who are unwilling to work together on their finances. When we first began to help people straighten out their finances, we taught one partner the system with the understanding that that person would, in turn, teach the principles to his or her spouse. Believe it or not, that method always made the situation worse. We were wasting precious time.

We do not counsel couples who are unwilling to work together on their finances.

I remember a couple who we tried to help. The husband was not in agreement with his wife's efforts to be debt-free. He accumulated debt as fast as she could pay it off. He purposely sabotaged her success. His actions only led to her frustration. She gave up after three months of taking one step forward and two steps back. The worst part of it all is that she felt like a failure.

This experience made it mandatory that for me to help them, both husband and wife have to be ready for change. Both spouses must be present at each meeting. They have to be 100% responsible and actively engaged in helping to turn their situation around. It is impossible to counsel couples who do not operate as a unit. Each partner has to feel the pain of breaking the debt cycle. Feeling the pain will cause the husband and the wife to think twice before going back into debt. Besides, when both participate, both will walk away with a sense of accomplishment. If one spouse does all of the work, the other spouse will not be able to internalize or appreciate the success of escaping the bondage of debt. This would be similar to finding an Olympic gold medal on the street. Would you wear it? You probably would not. No joy would come from wearing the Olympic gold medal around your neck because you did not make the sacrifices that it took to win the medal.

> ***Harmony is pure love, for love is complete agreement. —***
> Lope de Vega

The Power of Two

After attending our Financial Freedom Workshop, Billy and his wife shared with us that they paid off over $33,000 of debt in one year. Billy was even laid off not once, but twice, during this time period. A written budget seemed to have saved them more money during his layoff. Acquiring knowledge in managing their finances and doing it in unison with his wife made a big difference. It was interesting listening to this couple. They did not know whether to be happy or sad about their recent triumph. Happy that they had paid off such a huge amount of debt in such a short period of time, or sad that they accumulated that much debt in the first place. They also confessed that their relationship grew tremendously over the last year. They now enjoy being in each other's company, as 97% of their arguments were financially related.

Building a Life Together

Setting financial goals together is critical for any marriage. You will not be successful with budgeting if you cannot agree on how the money should be spent. It will be virtually impossible to get any of your goals accomplished if the two of you are headed in opposite directions. On the other hand, if you agree to work together on your financial goals, you will achieve more. If either of you wants to spend money on an item that does not line up with your financial goals, the decision to leave it off the budget will be a simple decision. Arguments will then become unnecessary because eliminating an item will not be perceived as a personal attack.

...if you agree to work together on your financial goals, you will achieve more.

When the two of you begin to set financial goals together, realize from the start that you are not going to agree on all of them. Pick out the major goals that the both of you can agree on as a starting point. You will, in time, find that most of the goals you once disagreed on are no longer important. Old goals will be replaced with new ambitions. Quaneshala and I don't always agree about every single item on the budget, but we do agree to respect each other's opinion. We always center our financial decisions on the big picture.

When Quaneshala and I came up with our first budget, she insisted that we add to it the purchase of a certain kind of bottled water. She will not drink tap water if her life depended on it. I spent days trying to convince her that purchasing water each month was a bad idea. Finally I came to my senses and agreed that the bottled water should be added to the list. I came to this conclusion because a thorough examination of our budget suddenly brought something to my attention. I was letting $30 a month cause disharmony in our relationship. I may have had more of a reason for resistance if Quaneshala was requesting the installment of a $5,000 filtration system in the house, but that was not the situation. It would only take $30 a month to make her happy. We were in total agreement about everything else on the budget. I almost let bottled water stand in the way of our financial destiny.

Quaneshala now drinks filtered water because of a documentary she viewed on television about the chemicals that are used to make plastic bottles. I was happy when she made that decision. I hated carrying those cases of water from the store to our house every month. But what if, at the time of our beginning budget, I would have allowed that argument to get in the way of our other goals? We would have missed out on so many financial victories. You simply never know how circumstances will play out in life. It's a never-ending cycle of change. That's what makes living so exciting. You will be constantly adding and eliminating goals throughout your life as the two of you continue to grow together as a couple. Whatever goals you agree upon, always remember to keep the unity. In unity, there is strength.

You simply never know how circumstances will play out in life.

Developing a Win/Win Attitude

Marriage is not about getting everything you want. You should always focus on what works best for the both of you. Try this exercise. Take out two sheets of paper. Each of you take a sheet and write down the financial goals that you would like to, or need to, accomplish as a couple. Your goals can range anywhere from a 1-20 year time frame. When the lists are finished, compare both lists. Rewrite a new list on another sheet of paper with the goals you have in common. Your common goals will be the skeleton from which you make decisions. Whenever you make financial decisions from here on, review your list to make sure those decisions are aligned with your written goals in order to confirm that you are headed in the right direction. Over time, figure out a way to work each other's personal goals into the budget.

One of Quaneshala's goals was to take a family vacation to Hawaii. My goal was to buy another car. We both wanted to pay off our house. I suggested that we pay off the house first, go to Hawaii second, and then I would look for a car. Shortly after we paid off our house, my mother passed away. I ended up keeping her truck which took care of my desire for another car, so I was happy. We postponed our trip to Hawaii for a year because our priorities shifted to taking care of my brother and to handling my mother's estate after her death.

Experience Counts

When Quaneshala and I cannot reach a conclusion about something, the person with the most knowledge concerning a particular decision usually wins. An example is that I know more about cars. If one of our cars breaks down, I will fix it or find someone else to repair it. But I still keep the communication open with her about each decision I make during these car repairs. I inform her on every step I am about to take. Open communication with my wife has saved us a tremendous amount of money. She has run across coupons that proved invaluable to helping with the car repairs thereby cutting our expenses. Two heads are always better than one. A spouse can be very beneficial in helping you save money, so take advantage of the talents that the love of your life brings to the table.

A spouse can be very beneficial in helping you save money...

When it comes to grocery shopping, there are certain stores my wife prefers. The prices are higher yet the food is fresher. I had to realize that it is not always best to go for the cheaper price. These examples simply show how we make our decisions. These rules are not set in stone. We change them as the need arises, and this is what works for us for now. Find a system that works for the two of you. You can tweak it as you go.

The Big Picture

When looking over the budget together, scrutinize every item you buy. Decide which items are legitimate and which can be eliminated. Obviously, items such as food and rent must stay on the budget because you know you have to eat and have to have a place to live. However, are the golf games and the nail appointments necessary? I'm not advocating that you make the budget so tight you can't possibly maintain it. Give an allowance even if it is no more than $50 a month for each of you. The amount may vary depending on what stage you're on (e.g. Future Star, Mountain Climber, or Trend Setter). When I first started eliminating debt, I enjoyed a $10 a week allowance. Every weekend, I would treat myself by renting $1 DVD's and getting a $5 combo meal.

Make sure that every dollar has a purpose. Spending every dollar allotted guarantees that no money will be wasted. The smallest amount of waste can have a great impact over a period of time (remember the compounding penny). There are going to be items that the two of you will not agree on. That's actually great. You have similar interests, but you are still two different people. More than likely, that's what drew the two of you together.

Here's a word of advice: stay focused on your goals when going over the budget. This is why, as a couple, written goals can be a valuable asset. If you're on the Mountain Climber phase, the first priority should be getting out of debt. Once you become a Trend Setter, you will be able to adjust the budget to incorporate more personal items. Don't worry about how you're going to pay bills that are coming up months down the road. Spend the majority of your time dealing with one month at a time. Who knows, you may get an unexpected bonus at work to pay off that bill that you spent countless hours worrying about. The old saying is true that most people spend more time worrying about what *could* happen instead of on what has *actually* happened.

> ***When people are divided, the only solution is agreement.* —**
>
> John Hume

Ultimate Trust

Once you have agreed on how to spend every dollar on the budget, both individuals must stick to it. The budget is like a binding contract. Breaking this contract without first discussing your intentions with your partner will damage the relationship. Failing to communicate about the budget diminishes a small piece of trust in the relationship each time the approved budget is not respected by one or the other in the marriage. I have been in a number of meetings where one person does not stay within the guidelines of the agreed upon budget. When trust is missing, it's not uncommon to see other areas like respect and honesty missing from the relationship. How you do anything is how you do everything. The spouse who overspends does not realize how this practice is affecting his or her marriage relationship. Any relationship missing these key components is doomed for failure. It is impossible to have a sense of security within the relationship when two people are unable to trust each other to be faithful to the budget.

When trust is missing, it's not uncommon to see other areas like respect and honesty missing from the relationship.

Plan Before You Spend

When couples first start budgeting together, we suggest that they start off meeting a minimum of once a week to review their budget. Tracking your progress weekly will aid in making sure you are meeting your financial goals. If you find yourself straying off course, you can quickly readjust your spending and get back on track before too much time has passed. Please do not wait a month before making the necessary adjustment to your budget. Making minor corrections each week will encourage you to continue along the road of your new financial destiny. Success is planned, not automatic.

Work the Plan and the Plan Will Work

We once counseled a couple who were finally ready to get their finances in shape. This was the first time that they were budgeting together since their marriage. They were off to a good start the first few months into their new financial plan. They had experienced a few minor setbacks, but nothing that could not be solved with a few adjustments. Their first real hiccup came when they went on a weekend trip out of town. When they returned home we asked them about their trip and whether or not they were able to stay within their budget. They admitted that they had spent more than the money allocated for that particular trip. They were very discouraged. We consoled them for a minute then asked what they learned from this experience. How could they prevent overspending on their next trip? They started the blame game at first. Immediately we directed their attention back to focusing on a solution. Honestly, how is blaming each other for the problem ever a solution? It only leads to frustration because couples will not accept responsibility for sabotaging their budget.

They agreed, after taking a few seconds to think, that they should have taken out the exact amount they were planning to spend in cash instead of using their debit card for purchases. They realized that they would have had no choice but to stop spending once the cash had run out. Putting these systems into place would have kept them from overspending. We spent about ten more minutes coming up with several additional ways they could plan for the other trip they were about to take within the next two weeks. Their hope for becoming financially free was renewed at the end of our conversation.

They were eager to share the news of their success after returning home from their second trip. They were able to stay within their budget on this trip. No longer did they have to succumb to overspending while out of town. They understood that their plan worked because they worked their plan.

Budget Meetings

I have noticed that since I have created a space for unity and trust with our finances, Quaneshala loves having budget meetings with me. We literally get excited when it's time to go over the bills. She knows that she has a voice and that I value her input. We set aside time once a month to sit down and review our budget goals for that month. We constantly talk about upcoming events throughout the month in preparation of the next meeting. We have such remarkable conversations because of the fun we're having watching the future we dreamed of come to pass.

We set aside time once a month to sit down and review our budget goals for that month.

Our budget meetings were long in the beginning. We needed extra time to become accustomed to planning together. Since we have been doing this for several years, our meetings now only consume ten minutes of time. The meetings to plan the budget are simply a part of our monthly routine.

Each month's bills are usually the same with a few exceptions (e.g. birthdays, holidays, etc.). We also meet at the end of the year to go over our budget for the next year. This meeting takes a little longer than our regular meetings. We spend a lot of time checking to see if we are still on target in the pursuit of our goals. During this year-end meeting we also decide whether or not we would like to continue working on current goals or replace those goals with new ones. Once a goal has been reached, we take the money that has been freed up and immediately apply it to a new goal. This is a very important rule of thumb because you don't want to slip back into the old habit of wasting money. Remember, every dollar has to have a purpose. Don't hesitate to replace an achieved goal with a new one.

Budgeting Becomes Second Nature

I have found that couples are sure to succeed in reaching their financial goals once budgeting becomes their second nature. In other words, talking about the budget with your spouse becomes natural. Quaneshala and I have mastered this skill. It's not unlikely for us to talk about our budget several times before our scheduled meeting. We are consciously aware that meeting our financial goals is a daily process. I believe this is the secret to why our regular meetings are so short. We are constantly planning for upcoming and unexpected events. We bounce ideas off of each other on how to best handle a particular situation. Brainstorming together has

We are consciously aware that meeting our financial goals is a daily process.

proven to be very beneficial over the years. Our meetings are mostly reserved for pulling a final decision from the potential solutions we've already discussed.

One Account Manager at a Time

It's very important to designate a person to pay routine bills out of the main account. Couples who share this responsibility quickly find out that a failure to communicate with each other about what has been spent can cause overdrafts and annoying costly fees. When only one spouse is responsible for the account, pending transactions made by the other person are non-existent. Arguments are then avoided.

One person should handle the literal paying of the bills. The question is, "Who should do it?" That question has an easy answer. The more disciplined of the two should be in charge of making sure all the bills are paid on time. Both of you, of course, should be involved in creating and finalizing the budget. However, only one of you should write the checks. The other person should serve as an accountability partner. The role of the accountability partner is to regularly check bank statements to ensure that only the items listed on the budget are being paid.

...only one of you should write the checks.

I have also known couples to take turns with this responsibility. If you like this suggestion, try switching roles from time to time. Find a system that works for the two of you. Simply make sure that someone is the assigned account manager.

Everybody's a Spender

When Quaneshala and I started budgeting together, I realized how different women and men think when it comes to spending habits. There has been a great debate for as long as I can remember about who spends more money, men or women. I personally believe that men and women spend money equally, but differently. Quaneshala can go to the mall and spend $30 a week on stuff. This does not seem like a lot of money until you look at the total at the end of the month. In four weeks, she would have spent $120. She spreads her spending out over a period of time so she does not consider herself to be a spender.

I, on the other hand, can spend the entire $120 dollars on one item and be just as happy. I don't have to make regular purchases on a weekly basis. I am not looking at how many times I can go shopping or how many items I can get with a certain amount of money. I can make one large purchase every so often and be content, while Quaneshala is satisfied with spending the same amount of money over a period of time. Do you see the difference? We're simply using different methods to do the same thing.

Forgiveness: Nothing Else Matters

Oftentimes one person in a relationship feels that he or she is better at budgeting than his or her spouse. Their strength in this area is unfortunately used as a power play against their partner. The focus in marriage, however, should be on finding ways to strengthen the relationship each and every day. What's the point in having a million dollars if your marriage is bankrupt?

A lot of couples have a hard time communicating and forgiving each other when their finances are in shambles. Communication and forgiveness are vital attributes in a healthy marriage. Your level of forgiveness will dictate how deeply the relationship can grow. Without forgiveness, communication is hindered. An unforgiving spirit will kill any chances of the two of you growing closer together as a couple. An inability, or an unwillingness, to forgive will cause unnecessary separation between you and your spouse. It is impossible for communication to flourish in this type of an environment.

Without forgiveness, communication is hindered.

Quaneshala and I are quick to forgive one another after having a breakdown in our relationship. We understand that disunity will block the love we share. I cannot feel the love in her touch, in her smile, and in her laughter when I, from my heart, refuse to forgive her. This lack of forgiveness also leaves room for the enemy to hinder our prayers. I am a totally different person when I do not walk in forgiveness. My spirit becomes cold, bitter, and selfish when I am not walking in the spirit of love. Very seldom will 24 hours pass before we forgive each other. We have come to understand that a house divided cannot stand.

A strong marriage must be preceded by the right kind of spousal conversations. Life and death is in the power of the tongue. Begin to speak life into your marriage and into your finances. Only then can transformation happen. Please pay attention to what I'm saying. I am certainly not saying that you should allow your spouse to take advantage of you based on their knowledge of your dedication to forgiveness. What I am saying is that you should spend more time focusing on building your spouse up instead of tearing your spouse down. It's mandatory that you get to the point in your relationship where nothing is more important than making the relationship work. If something in the marriage needs to be changed, then change it! Get a new attitude about your marriage relationship. You cannot let anything stand in the way of your marital unity. This may mean killing your pride in favor of submitting to your partner. An open mind and a willing heart can raise your relationship to higher heights. Go for it!

An open mind and a willing heart can raise our relationship to higher heights.

Time is a Virtue

Shortly before I married, one of my friends gave me some advice that I will never forget. He related to me the fear of telling his mother about his decision to get married. My friend's parents divorced when he was younger. He thought that his mother would perhaps disagree with his decision to marry based on her distasteful experience with his dad. He was certain that she would convince him to reconsider marriage.

He finally mustered up the courage to confide in his mom about his upcoming nuptials and discovered, to his pleasant surprise, that his mother was happy that her son had found someone special. He was startled by her reaction. She revealed that she and his dad were young and immature when they married. His parents are now really good friends after many years of divorce. She admitted that, over time, he eventually transformed into the man she originally wanted. She confessed to wishing that she had been a little more patient in waiting for the change. She wonders now what life could have been like had they stayed together and stuck things out.

You, as a couple, are starting the process of working together on your financial goals. Use my friend's story about his parents as a symbol of hope. Don't give up. A lot of couples can relate to the costly mistake made by my friend's mother. Two people gave up on a relationship before it had time to grow into a proper unit of love and strength. The couples who stuck together through thick and thin are so glad they did. Their future is a whole lot brighter because they hung on together. It takes a strong level of commitment to stay married in today's society.

However, I do believe that there are some cases, situations, and circumstances in which couples should part. I do believe, though, that those cases are few. Change is possible; it just happens over a period of time. We must be patient with others because it is certainly our desire for them to be patient with our own shortcomings. Don't allow impatience to rob you. A failure in patience opens the door to unreached goals. It takes faith to hold on to promises. If your spouse was good enough for you to marry, that same person is good enough for you to fight to keep. All things are possible with our God! My challenge to you is to weigh the cost of giving up. Think of the long-term effects of every decision you make. What's the price of that decision? Are you willing to pay the price?

Change is possible; it just happens over a period of time.

> ***Too often we underestimate the power of a touch, a smile, a kind word, a listening ear, an honest compliment, or the smallest act of caring, all of which have the potential to turn a life around. —***
>
> Leo Buscaglia

Just for Men

While you are going through the process of working on the finances together, give your wife a lot of selfless support. The reason I call it "selfless" is because you are not looking for anything in return. Your only intentions are to help her remain encouraged throughout the process and to show her that you care. Let her know constantly that you are cheering for the two of you to make it. She needs to feel secure in the fact that everything is going to be alright. Your wife needs to be able to depend on you to lead your marriage in the right direction. Over time the tides are sure to turn in your favor. Instead of paying off debt, you will begin to build wealth. When the wealth starts to build, don't touch it. Resist the temptation to run off and spend your entire savings on an impulse. Surely you have learned from past mistakes that a lack of money causes worry and stress. Most women interpret money as security. Give them that security. Anything less will forfeit your chances of a happy home.

Just for Women

Women, you also have a very important role to play in your marriage concerning the finances. Align yourself with your spouse in the arena of finances. This is especially true when finances are tight. Your first reaction might be to whine and complain about the situation. Strongly resist the urge to complain as it will only make matters worse. Find ways to build your husband up instead of looking for ways to tear him down. The enemy's job is to break unity within the relationship; don't offer him any help. Satan will try to knock you and your spouse off of the same page. If he can get your focus off of the primary goal, he wins. His goals are to steal, kill, and destroy. He works in the areas of your weaknesses. If it's the finances, he will attack there. Refute the enemy's attack by speaking words of life into your husband's spirit. It's imperative that you recognize demonic, but clever, tactics. You can't afford to let the devil win. Stand strong and firm. Pray with your husband. Use this opportunity to develop into the virtuous woman who God had called you to be.

The enemy's job is to break unity within the relationship; don't offer him any help.

Search for the Honey

I have found that couples are more willing to work together when each spouse shows appreciation toward the other spouse for the things that are already being done right in the relationship. Try to focus on all of the reasons why you married each other in the first place. There must be a reason why you chose to leave everyone else and to cling to your mate. When you fill your mind with thoughts of appreciation, you will come to a quick realization that your situation is not so bad that it can't be repaired. You may even begin to see that the two of you make an unstoppable team. Take the time and learn how to work together. Working together does not only apply to your finances, it applies to each area in your life. God will help you when you, as a married couple, decide to trust Him.

Magic Moments

I bought journals for us on our first wedding anniversary. The goal is for us to write in it once a month to capture and remember the beautiful moments we share with each other throughout the years. The 16th of every month is when we decide on a topic and record our thoughts. Once we are finished writing, we read what we have written to one another. I can't express how powerful these moments have been for us. It has given me a deeper understanding of how she feels about sharing a life with me. I am truly amazed at how our relationship has grown from such an easy exercise.

Every time we face a challenging roadblock in our marriage, we take out our journals and read about all of the other times we faced similar situations...

Every time we face a challenging roadblock in our marriage, we take out our journals and read about all of the other times we faced similar situations, but made it through okay. I had forgotten about some of those moments until recently when I picked up my journal and read about the past victories we shared. Sometimes we even laugh about how we let paper tigers masquerading as fears disrupt our unity. The only thing to fear is fear itself. Keeping a record of our past has provided exceptional breakthroughs in our relationship. We began to see our response pattern when faced with certain situations. I seriously believe that Quaneshala and I have saved years of heartache by taking the time to write those moments down in our journal. Each recording renews our hope that everything will work out for our benefit. Although problems continue to arise in our marriage (as they do in all marriages), we are confident that we can solve our problems together.

Create with Words

I love it when Quaneshala tells me the story of how we first met from her perspective. It seems as though she has told me the story a thousand times, but I still love to hear her tell it. I love to hear her speak of falling in love with me. I can just think of her words and become rejuvenated with the chemistry I share with her.

We also play a game called "Three Reasons Why…." You can fill in the space with whatever your heart desires. Some examples can be three reasons why you married me, love me or chose to spend the rest of your life with me. We spend 5 – 15 minutes twice a month on this exercise. I may say that I love her thoughtfulness, then I will explain what I mean by that statement. I may also mention the fact that I love how she gets up every morning and prays with me. This exercise helps us two ways. One, it lets my wife know how I feel about some of the things she does for me. Secondly, it also reinforces positive behavior by encouraging and inspiring her to keep doing what makes me happy.

One time after doing this exercise with Quaneshala, I spent an entire week experiencing joy and overwhelming excitement.

She told me that she looked up to me and that I was her hero. I was so floored by her comment because I often wondered what she really thought of me. I knew she loved me of course, but I desired to know her deepest emotions about me and about her thoughts concerning our relationship together. I try so hard to be the man of her dreams. I was unsure if I was meeting the mark I had set for myself until she revealed to me her innermost feelings. When she spoke those words, I knew all of the sacrifices I have made to please her have been worth it.

Please remember, whether you realize it or not, there is life and death in the power of the tongue. Ask yourself this question. Are you giving or taking life with the power of your words? If Quaneshala's words were able to change my emotions for an entire week, what effect do you think you could have on your mate by speaking positive words to them? You don't have to try to figure out the right thing to say. Start by simply encouraging them in some area where they may be struggling. Today, say something nice *to* them *about* them. You will soon develop a habit of speaking positive words. Small rocks make big ripples. Quaneshala made a lasting impression in my life that day. I no longer have to guess whether or not I'm her hero. I know I am because she spoke the words.

Please remember, whether you realize it or not, there is life and death in the power of the tongue.

Who Are You Following?

Orlando decided to change his profession and become a classroom teacher several years ago. He found his job of working with young, impressionable minds to be very rewarding. The only problem with the new job was the principal of the school. She gave him a hard time even though he was only a first year teacher. He already had a steep learning curve in his new profession, and having a principal constantly on his back made things worse. Her unrealistic expectations of him were affecting his attitude. She found every possible opportunity to tear him down. One year under her leadership took away his desire for another year in education. He thought about quitting all the time and considered finding a new job somewhere else. He didn't want to entertain this option as he found working with children to be very satisfying.

Orlando transferred to another school at the end of the year. His new principal was the exact opposite of his former principal. Orlando's new principal signed him up to be the Team Lead after only a few days at the new school. Orlando was shocked. It was hard to believe that someone he had known for just a few days trusted him with such a great responsibility. And Orlando had limited teaching experience!

There is more. Orlando was given more leadership responsibilities as the semester continued. He was invited to sit in on interviews for new hires and for other campus projects. His opinion was valued by his leadership team. Orlando received a new outlook on education because his new principal chose to focus on helping Orlando to develop into a leader instead of focusing on the skills Orlando lacked. This new principal encouraged him to dream big. He recommended that Orlando take a Masters Degree Program the district was offering. When Orlando obtains these credentials, he will be in a better position to pursue a future in administration.

What changed to bring Orlando all of this success? The only thing that changed was the leadership Orlando worked under. Orlando's superior was the key to his success. Herein is another super important point. It doesn't matter how much potential you have, hanging around the wrong people will hinder your growth. A different principal at a different school led to making a difference in Orlando's career. He went from being just another harassed teacher to a well-respected educator.

It doesn't matter how much potential you have, hanging around the wrong people will hinder your growth.

Compare Orlando's ordeal to your marriage. Will you be the one to hold your marriage back with your negative attitude, mean words, and bad spending habits? Decide today to focus on the great qualities of your spouse. Sure, your spouse has flaws. We all do. So do you. Your responsibility is to encourage them to achieve their full potential. The way you view your spouse, and the way you act toward your spouse, has the power to transform your marriage the same way Orlando's new principal transformed Orlando's career.

Trying to Always Be Right Can Leave You Dead Wrong

Winning an argument is not as important as unity with your partner. Look at it this way. Imagine you are driving home after a long day at work. While sitting at a red light, you see a semi- tractor/trailer truck approaching the intersection. All of a sudden, the traffic light turns green for you to proceed into the intersection. Before you step on the gas, you notice that the driver of the semi-truck is still approaching the intersection at full speed. What do you do? Should you drive into traffic now because you have the right of way or should you wait until the semi-truck passes before continuing your ride home? The answer should be obvious. Wisdom dictates that you wait until the intersection is clear before driving further. Waiting for the semi-truck to pass could save the life of the driver of that vehicle as well as your life—even though you had the right of way. You should always evaluate the possible outcome before making big decisions. It would not have been worth potentially losing your life just to prove to the driver of the semi-truck that you had the right away. Your only objective should be to make it home safety.

You should always evaluate the possible outcome before making big decisions.

This may not seem like a reasonable comparison, yet this is the way most people treat their relationship with their spouse. They spend more time trying to be right in every instance instead of spending more time on developing a powerful relationship with their spouse. They don't recognize the high cost of operating in pride. If this is a portrayal of you, begin to show your spouse that your main objective is for the two of you to achieve your financial goals together. Cover their areas of weakness with love. Praise them for the small changes they make. Always express yourself in a loving and considerate way. This will help you prevent unnecessary heartache and stress. Treat them like you would want to be treated. Remember the old saying: "You can catch more flies with honey than with vinegar."

I told my wife how to get my attention anytime she needs

something from me and I am not responding to her needs. In the past, she would communicate with me ineffectively. The methods she used to get my attention only pushed me away from her instead of drawing me closer. She now lies in my arms and puts her head on my chest. Then, using soft, positive words, she lets me know what she would like for me to do. When she approaches me in that manner, she reaches my heart every time. My undivided attention belongs to her. Love conquers all.

> ***You will be the same person in five years as you are today except for the people you meet and the books you read. —***
> Charles Jones

Be A Student

Personally, I love being a student of wealth. This fact may be the main reason I was so passionate about this book coming to fruition. I could not think of a better way than this to help others avoid the mistakes I made with money.

I have read books, listened to encouraging audio discs, and watched inspirational speakers teach on DVD about the subject of finance. This has blessed me with a wealth of information and ideas over the years. I absorbed all the material I could get my hands on. I used a lot of the information I collected to propel my life forward. I achieved success because I filled my mind with valuable material. I'm always left with feelings of inspiration and faith whenever I saturate my mind with lessons learned from those who have gone before me. Self-education helps me achieve the impossible.

It is critical that we feed our minds if we are to reach and fulfill our potential. We die when we refuse to grow. I enthusiastically encourage you to read books and articles that will challenge you to "*Think and grow rich*", as Napoleon Hill would suggest. Instead of picking up the television remote, pick up a book. A book that you have not read cannot help you. Just as important, feeding your mind will also help other people. You probably possess within you key information that someone else needs to utilize in their life.

Please don't let laziness keep you from leaving an unforgettable mark in someone's life.

Quaneshala and I always share articles and stories with each other about a wide variety of topics. Our pleasure of reading and learning empowers us with intellectual conversations and more time spent in each other's company. We challenge each other regularly with intriguing debates. These debates have taught me what Quaneshala values most. We start off discussing one topic only to end up entangled in a completely different but meaningful discussion. We have shared some intimate conversations that I will cherish for the rest of my life. These moments were created only because we decided to expand our minds and challenge each other to think. Please don't let laziness keep you from leaving an unforgettable mark in someone's life.

Start the Day Off with a Prayer

Quaneshala and I pray every morning before I leave for work. In our prayer, I ask for love, trust, communication, commitment, and prayer to grow stronger in our relationship. Below is a breakdown of why I have chosen these specific words to pray every day:

Love – love reminds us to always cherish one another because our days on earth are numbered. Love also helps us to forgive quickly because our Heavenly Father forgave us.

Trust – trust keeps us honest in our actions when we are away from one another. We don't want anything to jeopardize the companionship we have built over the years.

Communication – communication simply means that we are to always communicate with each other if there is a problem. We don't run to others asking them to solve our problems. There is no need to bring a third party into a situation. We can settle it ourselves by coming together and talking about it.

Commitment – commitment means that we are both committed 100% to making this marriage work. This includes having to sometimes swallow our pride. Regardless, we are there for each other.

Prayer – prayer is only last on this list, but it is definitely not last in our lives! Prayer is the key ingredient that makes our marriage work as well as it does. Some situations are changed only by prayer. When our own waywardness gets in the way of us doing what is right, we turn to Jesus. He knows how to work things out for the good of everyone involved.

All of these qualities must exist in every relationship, but the quality I would like to focus on is trust in the area of finances. Couples must be able to trust each other with their worldly goods. A woman especially needs to know that her husband is not going to go out and spend their life savings on a whim. Money saved in the bank gives women a sense of security. Women like to rest in the fact that, should an emergency happen, the household will still survive due to savings. Setting your finances in order will help to set your marriage in order by causing other things to run smoother. When trust is nowhere in the picture, unnecessary strain is placed on the relationship.

Setting your finances in order will help to set your marriage in order...

When I married Quaneshala, she was not 100% sure if she could trust me in the handling of our money. In the back of her mind, she suspected that I would wake up one day and go on a spending spree with our life savings. I can sympathize with her feelings of distrust. She did not grow up around men who were exactly financially astute. We were about a year into managing our money together before she finally realized that I was not going to do anything stupid with our money. All of our financial decisions are made together. We do not spend money without first discussing the expenditure with each another. Quaneshala's financial trust in me has opened up other doors in our marriage. Our relationship cannot grow any higher than our level of honesty and trust one for the other. My wife is aware that there is nothing too personal for us to share. Our relationship would not have grown to this higher level had I not proven my financial savvy to her. It would be quite foolish of me to trade in her hard-earned trust for a shiny trinket or some other unneeded item.

No Secrets Please

We were watching a movie together one day. The plot was about a couple divorcing after many years of marriage. Prior to the divorce, the husband found out that his wife had been hiding money from him. The husband was hurt because his wife had not been totally honest with him. The wife, though, felt that because she earned the money, it belonged to her. I then began to wonder if Quaneshala was hiding money from me. I immediately dismissed the thought and finished the movie. Quaneshala expressed after the movie that she was glad she did not have to hide or steal money from me. She admitted that the woman was wrong to keep secrets from her husband. Perhaps that was the reason for their divorce. I was very relieved to hear that Quaneshala felt no need to hide money from me.

I agreed with the husband in the movie. His wife should have been honest about the money she was hiding. I grew up hearing women advising other women to hide money from their husbands. I accepted that as a common practice in marriages. I'm married now so I can disagree with this ill advice. Women should never be placed in a position to feel a need to hide money for their private use. There is nothing wrong with a wife or a husband setting aside money for their personal use. However, the money should not be a secret kept from their spouse.

Stay Under the Covering

We have a main account that both of our checks go into each month. We pay bills out of this account. We also have separate checking accounts where we transfer our monthly allowances. If we have to purchase something for the house, we take it out of the main account. We use our individual accounts to buy personal items. We have given each other the freedom to make purchases with our personal account without discussing it with the other. Quaneshala is more than welcome to spend her money on whatever her heart desires. The same goes for me. It has nevertheless been very beneficial to discuss with each purchasing items that cost more than $100. It's not about giving each other permission; it's about watching out for one another. We run our more expensive purchases by one another for the sake of discussion.

I flew to the city of Orlando, Florida, one year to attend a conference. I needed an airline ticket, a hotel room, and a rental car. Any attempt to acquire these amenities without Quaneshala's advice would have resulted in a large loss of money. She is a master when it comes to bargain hunting for airfare. She found me a round trip ticket, a hotel, and a rental car for around $350. Two heads are indeed better than one.

There was also an occasion when one of Quaneshala's friends needed to borrow some money. We usually just give the money to the person if we feel it's for a worthy cause. Relationships tend to change with the people when you loan them money (we will discuss more on this in the next level). Quaneshala discussed her friend's predicament with me. I gave Quaneshala some sound advice which prevented this friend from attempting to take advantage of her in the future. Quaneshala did not need my permission to give her friend the money. Still, my advice saved my wife from having future problems with this same situation. In this case, it was not a worthy cause, so Quaneshala did not give her friend the money.

Take the Next Step

If you have made it this far on your journey to financial freedom, you are a dedicated student. Many people purchase a book but never read it, or they fumble through the first couple of chapters, put it down, and move on to something else. You didn't do that. You pushed through and made it to the end of Level 3.

Levels 1 – 3 gave you a wealth of information to transform your financial destiny. If you put into practice the principles outlined in this book, you will, without doubt, achieve financial success. You have been given the right tools to change your family tree. We have poured our hearts and souls into this book to ensure that each reader will have the secrets to mastering wealth. The steps for financial abundance have been explained in an easy to understand plan. Apply them to your life. It is your right to share in the abundance God has made available to all of us.

If you are ready for the next step, keep reading. It will blow your mind. The ultimate secret to wealth lays on *The 4th Level to Financial Freedom.*

> ***Live a life worthy of the calling you have received. —***
> Ephesians 4:1 NIV

LEVEL 4:
TRUE ABUNDANCE

We have laid out the proven strategies that will help you take control of your finances. You now have the potential to accumulate a massive amount of wealth that can be passed on to future generations. Reaching the 3rd level of financial freedom is a major accomplishment and is worthy of pride. You have lived a life like no one else and now it's time for you to reap the benefits. Most people only aspire to reach the 3rd level of financial freedom within their lifetime, but hold off on getting too excited about reaching the 3rd level; there is more to accomplish.

REACH FOR MORE

If you have made it to this level, you are really now in a position to make a difference. You have the money to give to organizations, people, and to causes that you believe in. The first three levels of this book focused on leaving a legacy for your children's children. This 4th level will focus on leaving your mark on the world. Since you have become financially free, the changes you can make in our society are immeasurable. The possibilities are endless.

THE 4th LEVEL EXPLAINED

Few people, as a way of life, experience living on *The 4th Level of Financial Freedom*. My wife and I consider the *4th Level of Financial Freedom* to be the most important section of this book. The financial resources that God has given you to steward can help you leave your imprint on this world. Your financial generosity will have an impact on the lives of countless other people.

I strongly believe that we are all put here on this earth to be givers of our time, our talent, and our treasure. Helping others is a purification of the soul. Giving is the reason we feel so rewarded on the inside after contributing to a worthy cause. Most people have mastered the art of giving their time and talent. We have dropped the ball, however, when it comes to sharing our treasure. There are many needs in the world that are yet to be fulfilled because of a lack of capital. You can probably think of projects in your own neighborhood that need financial support.

It's time for us to give not only our time and talent, but also our treasure (money). We make a difference by giving; it's the ultimate thrill of life. We need to take a stand and be the change we would like to see. Let's remember the words of John F. Kennedy, "... ask not what your country can do for you; ask what you can do for your country."

OPEN YOUR EYES

The reason we saved giving for the last level is because most people reading this book may not be in a financial position to give at this time. People who are in a bad financial situation must first be helped before they can shift their focus to helping others. We learned this from Maslow's hierarchy of needs. The Bible teaches us that as Christians, it is our responsibility to take care of the needs within our own household. When the needs of our personal household have been met, we should focus on the needs of other people.

THE BLIND SPOT

One afternoon, I called my friend Chris to check on him and his family. He informed me that his financial situation was not good. I immediately consoled him with the same secrets that are outlined in this book. He was very excited about the first three levels. His excitement dwindled when I began talking about *The 4th Level of Financial Freedom.* My friend's load of debt was so heavy he could not fathom the possibility of financially blessing anyone else. His exact words were, "You were doing well until you started talking about giving money away." His current financial lack blinded him to the purpose of wealth. When you have an abundant supply, you don't mind parting with some of that supply; you understand the giving and receiving principle. I realized that Chris would not be able to comprehend the importance of *The 4th Level of Financial Freedom* until he mastered the 1st, 2nd, and 3rd levels.

Take a look at the supply and demand theory. Pretend that you love chocolate candy bars. If you had only one of your favorite bars in possession, you would probably be less likely to share it with anyone. The demand for the chocolate candy bar would be great and the supply would be low. However, if you had 1,000 chocolate candy bars, you would be much more willing to share them. The demand would be low and the supply would be high. Money works the same way. People who have more than enough money to take care of their own needs generally don't mind sharing money with others. Everyone doesn't follow after the selfish, greedy characteristic of Ebenezer Scrooge before his redemption. They are quite the opposite of him.

> ***...The amassing of wealth is one of the worse species of idolatry. No idol more debasing than the worship of money. —***
>
> Andrew Carnegie

TRUE ABUNDANCE

People who are walking in true abundance love to share their wealth. If I can borrow the words of Barney, the purple cartoon dinosaur, I would say, "Sharing is Caring." Stingy people are usually lonely and unhappy people. True happiness and freedom are expressed when you share. It's like a child that sticks his hand in a candy jar. When he reaches in and grabs all of the candy, he soon finds out that his hand is too full to remove it from the jar. The large possession of candy has expanded his hand, making it too big to pull back through the opening of the jar. His hand will only be free when he releases some of the candy. Sharing is a great lesson for children to learn as early as possible so that they will realize there is enough to go around for everyone.

Sharing is a great lesson for children to learn as early as possible so that they will realize there is enough to go around for everyone.

Another friend of mine, whom I'll call Jeff, purchased a house and invited me over to see it. It was a very nice home. The inside was decked out with big screen TV's, an entertainment system, a drum set, computers – the list goes on and on. His "Man Cave" was filled with a lot of cool toys that any guy could appreciate. I began to notice a pattern while touring his house. He spent a lot of time showing off his trinkets, but he never did offer me any opportunities to play with his "toys." I spent most of my time watching him play; he was having a ball. I literally watched him hammer away on his drum set for 30 minutes. It was a boring visit and I could not wait to leave. I was not looking forward to another invitation to Jeff's home. There is no enjoyment in watching someone else have all the fun. I wish my friend would have realized that our time together would have been better spent if only he would have shared.

THE BENEFITS OF GIVING

Jesus stated some powerful words in the gospel of Luke. He said, "For unto whomsoever much is given, of him shall be much required." Wealth brings with it a responsibility, not to be feared, but to be a catalyst for change. Your compassion in the area of giving can alter someone's life for the better.

Your compassion in the area of giving can alter someone's life for the better.

There are countless benefits that accompany the ability and the willingness to give. Today, people are seeking happiness and joy in various places—oftentimes in the wrong areas. Those happy emotions can actually come about as a result of sharing. What can bring you any greater joy than knowing that your money brought a homeless family off the streets? How blessed are you when you are able to pay for a child's operation because the parents don't have insurance or any other monetary resources? It has been said that money can't buy happiness. That's debatable, so let's just say that money does provide choices for you and for others.

Spreading wealth around where it's needed builds character; promotes selflessness; proves that love is still alive; inspires other people to give; and helps you focus on solving the problems of others. You may not look for a return of your giving, but a return is inevitable. That is the law of sowing and reaping.

Nevertheless, I do not give to gain the benefits; I give because it is the right thing to do. I grew up receiving from other people and was grateful for their generosity. It's heartwarming knowing that there are still those who care and share. The benevolence of others over the years has conditioned me to pay it forward.

$1,000 CHALLENGE

Perhaps you're still not convinced that it is rewarding to give. Okay. Try this exercise. Take $1,000 and sit it on a table next to you. Take a piece of paper and write down a list of ways you could spend $500 dollars on yourself. What would you buy? Spend every cent. Next, make another list of ways you could spend $500 on a person, or persons, that would drastically change their life. Think of all the people you know that are experiencing tough financial times.

When the lists are complete, take $500 and spend it on yourself and take the other $500 and spend it on someone according to what you have written on your second list. Write a paragraph about how you felt after completing this exercise. I sincerely believe that you'll find that spending money on yourself was not as rewarding as helping someone else in need. Buying "*things*" will only bring about temporary satisfaction. The thrill of self-gratification does not last very long. The only way to experience fulfillment on this earth is to impact the lives of others.

> ***...He which soweth sparingly shall reap also sparingly; and he which soweth bountifully shall reap also bountifully. —***
>
> 2 Corinthians 9:6

THE MISCONCEPTION ABOUT GIVING

You are now in a position to give, yet you must also be guided as to when and where to give. It's a blessing to be able to give, but sadly you will eventually discover that you cannot give to every cause in the world. If you attempt this action, you will soon deplete your funds and find yourself back at square one. That would be devastating. Besides, if you're trying to do all of the giving, you have obviously forgotten that it is the responsibility of others to also give. Everyone must strive to make a difference in their family, their community, and in the world around them. We all have a part to play. Giving and sharing is not just for the rich or for those who are financially stable. It is a humane duty. The amount of money, time, or whatever it is that's being given is measured by the motive of the heart more than the size of the gift.

There are legitimate times when, and reasons why, you should not give to certain needs. Quaneshala and I have turned down the opportunity to help family and friends on many occasions. Several times we have chosen not to give because the individual needing our help expected us to make all the sacrifices while they stood on the sideline watching. That raised a red flag for us. We don't help people who don't try to first help themselves. Another reason we have refused to give is because it would have put us in a vulnerable position. We perhaps had enough money to cover their need, but supplying that need would have depleted our funds. What if an emergency would have risen in our lives afterwards? We would have been in some serious trouble. We certainly could not have asked others for help because they were looking to us for their own assistance!

We don't help people who don't try to first help themselves.

We have to use wisdom when making our giving decisions. We want to give out of our abundance—not take from our monthly bills, retirement accounts, emergency fund, etc. We know of people who gave money that was supposed to be set aside for their retirement. Twenty and thirty years later, those same individuals were disheartened to learn that they had not saved enough money to sustain their living expenses for their retirement years. What a harsh reality to face. You can avoid this pitfall by only giving from your overflow. Here is an idea. Decide on a certain amount to give for each month of the year. Once you have given out that amount, stop giving until the next month. Find a balance that works for you.

When it comes to giving, you can also look into alternatives. Check to see if your company offers programs that give to organizations for which you already volunteer. A lot of companies have money specifically set aside to give, but their employees do not take advantage of those available funds. Quaneshala and I always think outside of the box in terms of our giving. When we're out eating at a restaurant and have extra coupons, we share them with the other diners. I'm sure we have helped others save hundreds of dollars with little effort on our part. Never forget, when done the right way, giving on any level will turn out to be a blessing for all involved.

WHEN TO GIVE

Please don't be misled into thinking that you should give only *after* reaching *The 4th Level of Financial Freedom*. Generally, a person that has reached this level has had a little more time to accumulate more wealth. However, a situation may occur that requires your help before you have reached the 4th level. Whatever your financial status is at any given time will dictate the amount of money you contribute to a cause.

There were a couple of occasions during my debt elimination program when I gave some money to friends and family to meet a critical need. Those times, though, were few and far between. I did not give just because someone came crying for help. I had to decide whether or not the need was worthy of my support because my first priority was to free myself from the bondage of debt. You will create a distraction by trying to accomplish too many goals at once. You can't live a lifestyle of perpetually giving away money while also eliminating debt. One plan has to trump the other.

You can't live a lifestyle of perpetually giving away money...

Here is a suggestion if you have not yet reached *The 4th Level of Financial Freedom*, but have a heart to give. Make a list of causes/organizations to which you would like to donate upon reaching *The 4th Level of Financial Freedom*. Once you have reached the 4th level, start setting money aside to donate to these causes. This list may also provide you with an extra incentive to reach the 4th level.

How do you decide when it is appropriate to give? It's a legitimate question. Deciding when to give can be challenging, especially when you're trying to be a wise steward over the money God has placed into your hand. We, as a married couple, constantly evaluate our financial decision to make sure we are in the perfect will of God. The Bible warns that the ***love*** of money is the root of all evil. We consistently check our attitude about money and our relationship with it so as to keep it in its proper place. We have no desire to become high-minded because of the financial resources given to us of God. He owns it all anyway.

> ***Every man according as he purposeth in his heart, so let him give; not grudgingly, or of necessity: for God loveth a cheerful giver. —***
>
> 2 Corinthians 9:7

THE 12 PRINCIPLES OF GIVING

In this next section, you will discover how my wife and I give based upon 12 principles based upon our core beliefs. These principles help us determine the worthiness of a need. Please feel free to use these same principles as a guide or customize them to your situation during your times of benevolence. By no means are these principles written in stone. They are only suggestions.

GIVE FROM A PLACE OF POWER

Many people were left devastated after the destruction of hurricane Katrina. Family members, as well as possessions, were lost. People were without power, water, and food for days, even weeks before major assistance arrived.

Weeks after the storm, a friend told me a story about a guy and his gas can. Two days after Katrina's touchdown on the coast, this guy headed to a gas station to get some gas for his generator because the majority of the people were still without electricity. The guy ran into one of his neighbors on this trip who told the man how the storm had affected him and that he also needed a gas can. The neighbor asked the guy if he had an extra gas can. The guy, feeling sorry for his neighbor and without thinking, gave his neighbor his one and only gas can.

You are probably assuming that this was a noble thing for this guy to do. Giving his only gas can away to his neighbor was a kind act indeed. But answer this question: how is the first guy going to get his gas? His family was depending on him to return home with gas for their generator. The story ends with this guy spending the rest of the day running around town in search of another gas can to replace the one he gave away.

...sometimes people give out of their lack instead of from a place of power.

This story illustrates that sometimes people give out of their lack instead of from a place of power. The guy should not have given his neighbor the only gas can in his possession. He should have thought of a better solution that would have served them both. The neighbor could have waited to use the gas can after the other man finished refueling his generator. This was not a win/win situation.

Why do some people feel as though it's their sole responsibility to provide for everyone who has a need although they barely have enough? I call this, "Playing God." You can't give someone something that you don't have. It's frustrating trying to do so. The guy was not in a place of power when he gave away his only gas can. He only transferred the need. He became the one in need instead of his neighbor; therefore, the problem was not solved. Now if the guy had owned several gas cans, it would have been his moral responsibility to share with his neighbor. Unfortunately, he only had one. The safety and comfort of his family was supposed to be his number one priority.

Why do some people feel as though it's their sole responsibility to provide for everyone...

If a similar situation ever happens to you, please give only from a place of power. Don't give what you cannot afford to give. A justification of your sacrifice is nothing more than a poor financial decision. The scriptures declare that God will supply all of our needs according to His riches in glory by Christ Jesus. God will not use your lack to supply the needs of other people against you. He is a God of love and of wisdom. God has more than enough supply to meet the needs of everyone. I know this to be true from my own personal experiences with Him. God is faithful.

A LESSON ON GIVING FROM THE SQUIRRELS

Squirrels are remarkable creatures. There are a number of them that leap from tree to tree throughout our neighborhood. Quaneshala saw a squirrel digging holes in our back yard for the purpose of storing food. It is amazing how they are intelligent enough to prepare for the winter months by storing food ahead of time.

I am sure that squirrel is not going to invite all of the other squirrels in the neighborhood over to our back yard for a party the night before winter begins. A foolish decision like that would defeat his purpose and all of his hard work. Likewise, living on The 4th Level of Financial Freedom does not mean that it is perfectly okay for you to stop practicing all of the wisdom that you gained from the earlier lessons in this book. Money and resources will not stay in place accidently. Wealth must be maintained on purpose. The moment we deal with finance halfheartedly is the moment she will leave us for a stronger suitor.

GIVE TO SHOW LOVE

There are two commandments that are the greatest in the Law. The first commandment is to love the Lord with all of our heart, soul, and mind. The second commandment is to love our neighbor as we love ourselves. Financially, we can show God love, trust, and appreciation by giving Him our tithes and offerings. We can show love to ourselves by studying wealth to become financially independent. We can show love to our neighbors by using a portion of our abundance that God allowed us to accumulate to help people in need.

If you have made it to The 4th Level of Financial Freedom, great job! You are in the perfect position to show love through giving. If you are still on one of the other three levels of financial freedom, focus on reaching The 4th Level of Financial Freedom before fully expressing yourself through giving. Yes, you should give your tithes. Yes, you can help with critical needs that arise, but stick to only covering the basics until you reach The 4th Level of Financial Freedom. Please remember that you cannot fully love yourself when you give out of your lack. Your efforts to give will be premature.

When your electric bill is due is not the time to show benevolence to your neighbor. You must, at this time, show love to yourself. Love yourself enough to pay your electric bill so that your family will not suffer. There will be plenty enough time to show love to your neighbor when your financial situation improves. If becoming a brain surgeon is your career goal, would it be logical for you to perform a surgery on a person when all you have is a high school diploma? No one in his right mind will let you operate on him unless you have earned the proper medical credentials from the best universities. Anything less is experimenting with people's lives. You will only be considered a qualified doctor after decades of mastering your field of study. This may seem to be a drastic example, but there really is a time and season for everything (see Ecclesiastes 3:1). You can't give directions to others until you have traveled the road. Succeed in your endeavors first, and then you can be a hero in the life of someone else.

Succeed in your endeavors first, and then you can be a hero in the life of someone else.

GIVE TO SOLVE A PROBLEM

Whenever you give, make sure your financial resources will be used to solve a problem and not just eliminate the symptoms of it. Identify the real problem before giving to a cause; otherwise, you will have only wasted your financial resources. Throwing money at a problem will not automatically correct it. Find out what lies beneath that problem. You may find it hard to believe, but money is not always the answer to a need.

Never become an enabler. Running to the rescue of someone who repeatedly asks for money will not solve their problem(s). The real solution may be to teach the ones who always have their hands out how to manage their own money. People are empowered when you teach them how to fish, which results in feeding them for a lifetime instead of giving them a fish that will only feed them for one day.

The real solution may be to teach the ones who always have their hands out how to manage their own money.

Some parents are an example of contributing to a problem instead of solving it. They spoil their children. Children need to be disciplined in the matters of money and gifts. Giving a child everything he or she asks for is a future train wreck waiting to happen. Children without discipline are children out of control. Teachers, peers, employers, and ultimately, the police, will have trouble convincing those same children that the world and everyone in it was not created to serve them.

Parents, you do your children an injustice when you do not teach them, at an early age, the value of money and how they are responsible for earning and maintaining it as they grow older. The naked truth is that children would choose strong, attentive parents over the best gifts any day. In their heart of hearts, children want parents to fulfill their role as parents. They do not need an all season Santa Claus.

GIVE FOR THE RIGHT REASON

Some people give because they are worried about what others may say, feel, or think about them, but your opinion is what matters most. Jesus was without sin and they still crucified him. Do you expect people to have a merciful and kind opinion of you when you do not meet their requests for money? All you have to do is make sure that your motive for giving, or for not giving, is always a pure one.

Look for the causes that you are passionate about and support them. Never give to anything that contradicts your core beliefs. Does the purpose of the cause, the work, the organization, the charity, or the business, align with who you are as a person? Please do not allow anyone to force or persuade you to give to a cause that you just might regret participating in later. Give from the right place—your heart. It will guide you into making the right decisions. Listen to your inner voice. It was given to you to help you avoid traps, lies, and regrets.

It's amazing what can happen to and for you when you give for the right reasons. I have always profited directly or indirectly in some way as a result of giving. I shared earlier about how our company, The Heart of a Teacher, was started. We started out teaching our financial principles to the Sunday school class at the church where we were attending at that time. Three classes later, the pastor's wife enlightened us with the idea of getting paid to teach our classes. The rest is history.

We need each other. Sometimes you're the giver; sometimes you're the receiver of a gift. You can't live on an island by yourself and survive forever. Add joy to the lives of others. Show your family, friends, neighbors, and strangers that they are valuable not only to God, but also to you.

GIVE TO THE RIGHT CAUSE

Supporting the right cause can be very rewarding. There are a number of noble causes that are awaiting our attention. When we started researching people that have given to charities, the list was endless. One of the great leaders from the past that used his wealth to advance civilization was Andrew Carnegie. Carnegie donated most of his money to establish libraries, schools, and universities. Let's fast forward to the present. Billionaires like Warren Buffett and Bill Gates have pledged to give up most of their wealth to philanthropy. It's reported that Oprah Winfrey has given over $300 million dollars to various charities.

Ordinary people (individuals with modest income) are also benevolent with their money. A family sold their home and purchased another one, half the size, in order to donate half the proceeds to charity. Another lady shopped at rummage sales, walked everywhere she went, and lived in a one-bedroom house. No one would have ever realized that she was worth millions. When she passed away, she left her multimillion-dollar estate to her alma mater. We also heard of a couple who adopted two small children. They experienced an overwhelming joy from raising their adopted children which motivated them to find a way to help other families that were considering adoption, but lacked the financial resources. The couple started a foundation that raises money in order to offer grants to families seeking financial assistance for adoption.

When the cause is big enough, individuals take on the challenge and give of their finances to make a difference.

When the cause is big enough, individuals take on the challenge and give of their finances to make a difference. People will challenge themselves and make unreasonable financial commitments to accomplish remarkable goals if the cause is near and dear to their heart. The greatest gift is giving to the right cause.

A BLESSING FROM THE LORD

What a blessing! New Bethel Apostolic Assembly is a fairly new congregation, but ask any of its members about the goodness of God and they will tell you their amazing story.

It begins January 23, 2005. Pastor Thomas Lee Franklin, his wife Alice, and about five others began having services in the conference room at a local hotel in Moss Point, Mississippi. Things were going well until the hotel came under new management. The new management team wanted to charge them almost double the rent that they had been paying. Pastor

Franklin simply relocated to a different hotel. The congregation was growing. Pastor Franklin and his assistant pastor, Elder Ewing Lawson, began looking for churches that were for sale in the area.

In September 2005, the church had to leave the hotel conference room because the building was badly damaged by Hurricane Katrina. The members of New Bethel began to meet in Pastor Franklin's home. After much searching, the church began to use the Mid-Town Reunion Center in Moss Point as their temporary home. Services were held there for almost a year. However, God was working out a plan for His saints. That divine plan left their pastor crying tears of joy and the members of New Bethel Apostolic Assembly leaping and shouting and praising our mighty God for what He had done.

A member of New Bethel heard that a large church on Griffin Street in Moss Point was for sale and alerted Pastor Franklin. He and the executive board of New Bethel met with the Griffin Street Baptist Church to negotiate a price. While the negotiations continued, the members of New Bethel fasted and prayed that the Lord would bless them with their own place to call home.

In June 2006, a representative from Griffin Street Baptist came to where the members of New Bethel were having their church services and told the pastor that he had some good news for them. So, the pastor called the representative up front to tell the congregation the news. First, the representative whispered to the pastor, "Our church voted this morning to GIVE you the church." The pastor broke out in a shout and a loud praise. At that time, the congregation didn't know how good the news was, so once again Pastor Franklin told the representative to please tell the congregation what he just told him.

I can truly tell you they haven't stopped praising God yet. YES, it is true—they gave them the church. New Bethel now has the deed. Don't try to figure it out, just praise God with them. When your season comes, everything will be alright! The church was appraised for over $1,000,000. It came complete with instruments, kitchen appliances, furniture, etc., a seating capacity of 500 on the main floor and 60-70 in the balcony, 12 classrooms, two organs, two pianos, plus a library equipped with loads of books, along with food in the refrigerator and freezer. The church has seven restrooms and a "Welcome Center."

They had moved to different locations over the course of 18 months, but the members of New Bethel Apostolic Assembly, Moss Point, Mississippi, finally had a place to call HOME.

> ***Give, and it shall be given unto you; good measure, pressed down, and shaken together, and running over, shall men give into your bosom. For with the same measure that ye mete withal it shall be measured to you again.*** —
> Luke 6:38

GIVE AND TRUST

When we counsel our Christian clients about their finances, we find that most of them struggle with giving their tithes. This is a common problem in all churches. I was appalled when I found out that less than 3% of evangelicals give tithes. It's no wonder so many churches are closing due to lack of financial contributions. We teach individuals a simple technique on how to break their pattern of not giving tithes. The key is to start small and work your way up. Each individual's case is different, but here is one of the methods we have used in the past that works. Even if you are not a Christian, we still suggest that you think about giving at least a tenth of your income away to a charity.

During our first counseling session with clients, we strongly encourage them to put a category on their budget for tithes/giving even if it is only one dollar. You may be thinking, "One dollar?" Yes, $1. Don't despise the day of small beginnings. I know starting out this amount may seem small, but our goal is to slowly instill into clients the habit of tithing/giving. People don't change overnight. Criticizing them about their failure to give will not help the problem. We have to teach people how to become faithful in tithing/giving. In time, the seed of this process will grow.

We have to teach people how to become faithful in tithing/giving.

The amount given will increase with time and practice. The following month, we encourage them to increase the amount to 1% of their monthly income. The third month, we will encourage them to increase the amount to 5%. Each month we encourage them to continue increasing their contributions until they reach the Biblical requirement of 10%. We acknowledge their success throughout the process. We also take the time to explain to them why tithing/giving is so important because it teaches us to be grateful by realizing how blessed we are to be able to give. Over time, the individuals that begin to understand this concept are transformed into happy givers. Christian strength is an asset to the Kingdom of God.

GIVE AND FORGET

My original thought was that this topic is a no brainer. I found out, however, that no matter what subject is being taught, all ground must be covered. Stay away from people who believe their financial contributions are wholly responsible for your success. Abraham was wise enough to know better (Genesis 14:21-23). Abram refused to accept goods from the king because he did not want anyone, other than the Lord, taking credit for making him rich. If God blesses you to be a blessing to others, always keep in this truth in your heart: God gave you the resources. Heaven and earth belongs to the Lord.

Your giving should never be used to control the people who you help.

Your giving should never be used to control the people who you help. Pride will void the goodness of your deed and make the benefactor regret receiving help from your hands. Please don't wield some kind of false power over the people that you choose to aid. Give it and forget it. Why keep score? Why expect favors to be returned? Why brag about your benevolence? Someone had to help you along the way, too. You should be giving because God has been so good to you.

I have heard people talking about their liberality, and they are holding what they have given to an individual over that person's head. No one wants to hear you blow your own trumpet. Treat others the way you want to be treated. The tables have been known to turn. The person or people you help today may have to help you tomorrow.

GIVE TO SERVE

Some people fear the accumulation of wealth out of a fear of losing it all. They remember the story of Job and how he lost his wealth and his family. They conveniently forget about Job's ending. God returned to Job double of everything the enemy stole from him. I had a friend who constantly questioned my saving habit. She took pride in the fact that she spent every dollar she made. She asked what I would do if God commanded me to sell all of my possessions, give everything to the poor, and follow Him. She was of course making reference to the Bible's account of the rich young ruler in Luke 18:22. I responded, "I would at least have something to give."

It took a while to get enough courage to answer her question with confidence. I believe that everyone, at one time or

I believe that everyone... wonders about God's view of people's desire and efforts to build wealth.

another, wonders about God's view of people's desire and efforts to build wealth. I then began to realize three things which took the power out of her question. My first realization is that God does not give us the spirit of fear. Fear comes from Satan, the enemy of our souls. Second of all, God owns the riches of this world anyway. Everything is His to give and to take. Lastly, the Bible is laden with people who were blessed mightily by God with wealth and riches. Most people know about Solomon and his wealth. God gave Solomon an abundance of everything, and the man didn't even ask God for it! Solomon asked God for wisdom to know how to rule among His people. God granted Solomon's request and also added riches, fame, and honor to this king of Israel because Solomon's heart was in the right place—to first become a servant. His top priority was to serve God's people.

...God does not give us the spirit of fear. Fear comes from Satan...

GIVE TO THE BORROWER

When people borrow money, they become an automatic slave to the lender (Proverbs 22:7). My wife and I have loaned money to people so we understand well the relationship of master and slave. The borrower feels awkward whenever they are around the lender. An unpaid loan can ruin, or at the very least, alter, your relationship with the person(s) who owes you money.

Therefore, now when someone asks to borrow money from us, we simply give the money to them if we're in the financial position to give it and it is warranted. Some of our relationships with family and friends were salvaged because we chose not to be their master. The majority of the people who ask us for help usually have a serious need. I'm sure it took a lot of courage for them to even ask for our help. Asking for a helping hand is not as easy for some folks as it is for others. So, if a need is really there, you will feel good about pulling someone up from their lowest point.

We do practice paying it forward. We believe, however, in feeding the need, not the greed. We don't invest in a person's selfish desires. It's a true saying; money does not grow on trees. We don't give our money away to just anyone who asks. A real need is the only requirement that receives our attention and subsequent help. It's that simple.

GIVE WHEN GOD TELLS YOU

There are those who justify their misuse of money by bringing God into the equation. "God told me to do it." Did He really? I don't believe so. Your poor financial management is at fault, not God's faulty direction. God doesn't have faults and He doesn't mislead people.

Educate yourself about wealth. Stop blaming God for your lack. There are times when God will tell you to give. God sometimes led us to give although we did not understand at that particular moment the reason behind the giving. We had to let faith guide us.

God will try your heart. He wants to know what we're trusting—Him or money? In the early years of my spiritual growth, I attended a church convention in Memphis, Tennessee. During the service, I felt a calling from God to put $100 dollars in the offering. I was a college student at the time so that was a lot of money. I had reserved those dollars for other expenses. I sat in my chair for about fifteen minutes debating about whether God was speaking to me or not. I finally made up my mind to make the sacrifice and to trust in God. I carefully took a $100 bill out of my pocket and crumpled it up in my hand so no one would see what I was giving. When we were instructed to walk around for the offering, I grew a little more nervous about this sacrifice. While waiting for my turn, the friend who came with me to the convention put some money in my hand. Wow! The Lord provided a ram in the bush. This, I feel, was my first major test concerning my trust for God.

All of my tests from God concerning money are not always that easy. I end up giving the money in most cases. God's money tests have actually caused me to be more passionate about giving. Learn through my personal experiences. Giving will not always make sense. It is then that you must trust in, and depend on, the Lord's guidance.

Giving will not always make sense. It is then that you must trust in, and depend on, the Lord's guidance.

GIVE FOR THE KINGDOM SAKE

God has always touched the hearts of men to give, fulfilling his purpose for the Kingdom of God. The children of Israel are a great example of giving to the Kingdom. Donations were asked of the children of Israel for the building of the tabernacle in the wilderness. These people of God gave so much for that project that Moses had to tell them to stop giving! What a great problem to have! Envision charities all around the world having to turn down offers of money because too many financial donations had already come in and they had need of no more. Just imagine.

GIVE LIKE THE ULTIMATE GIVER

Jesus Christ is the ultimate giver. He is the best example we can follow when it comes to giving. Jesus gave His time, talent, and His treasure to others. Ultimately, Jesus gave His life. He purchased eternal life for us with His blood (John 3:16). The sacrificial death of our Lord Jesus Christ provided salvation to the world through a new birth of water and spirit. Now we give because Jesus gave.

The blessing of sharing your resources is only part of the privilege of serving God. There are countless other advantages to taking on the characteristics of The Ultimate Giver. Seek the Savior while he may be found. The rewards are greater than anything you have ever imagined.

> ***If you can't be generous when it's hard,***
> ***you won't be when it's easy.*** —
> Gordon Dean

PASTORING WITH A VISION

Pastor Wilson is a man of vision and faith. His church paid off several million dollars in debt. When he first became pastor, Pastor Wilson painted a clear picture to the congregation of what the church could accomplish if it was not deep in debt. Pastor Wilson believed that, with the right vision, his church could become debt-free. Out of debt, his church could have a greater impact on the community.

Pastor Wilson attributes the secret of his success to having a clear vision of a debt-free church. He felt that if the church was not paying thousands of dollars to the bank each month, the money could be used to build up the Kingdom of God in all capacities. The pastor urged the church members to contribute towards financial freedom. The people became excited and knew that it would take everyone's participation to successfully pay off the mortgage.

When people came to Pastor Wilson with questions about the new vision, he answered those questions honestly. The congregation believed in Pastor Wilson and they believed in his vision for the future of the church. They trusted their pastor to do what he said he would do with the money as it poured in—pay off debt. Well, today that church is no longer a slave to debt. The congregation gave generously and turned their dream into reality. They now have plans for church additions which will be paid for with cash. There is indeed strength in unity.

> ***It is a terrible thing to see and have no vision.*** —
> Helen Keller

$1 MILLION DOLLAR PROJECT

Our church is Better Way Apostolic Church in Arlington, Texas. My wife and I started the $1 Million Dollar Project to help raise money for our church. We became advocates for such a major project because we believe strongly in our pastor and in his wife, Dr. Harold and Shirley Durham. They're doing ground-breaking work in the community. They have been renting a facility for church services and community events for over fifteen years. They're grateful for what they have, of course, but it is our desire for our church to have a home of its own, and most importantly, we want to do it without incurring debt. We have purposed in our hearts to give of ourselves in order to achieve this remarkable goal.

Pastor and First Lady Durham are leaders with unbelievable passion for helping people transform not only the spiritual man, but natural man as well. Their motto is, "You have to touch the heart before you can touch the head." Our pastor and his wife understand that people don't care how much you know until they know how much you care. They are doing an excellent job fulfilling the vision God placed in their hearts. Some of the outreach ministries of the church include:

> **"You have to touch the heart before you can touch the head"**

- Abstinence Program
- Anger Management
- Back to School supplies give away
- Child Care
- Christian Counseling

- Financial Planning
- G.E.D. Preparations
- Inspirational Fitness
- Job Interviewing Skills
- Marriage Couple Fellowship
- Mentoring Youth Program
- Parenting Skills
- Seasoned Saint Fellowship (age 50+)
- Summer Feeding Program
- Family Pathfinders of Tarrant County

All of these are good works. A permanent location, however, will allow us to reach even more people in the community who are in dire need of help. Support would increase if our church owned its facilities. Some future ambitions are to provide:

- Transitional housing
- Food pantry
- Serve meals to the poor
- Christian school for grades K-12
- Bible College
- Faith Base Drug Program
- Counseling Center
- Resale Shop
- Technical School
- Beauty & Barber School
- Retirement Complex

If you feel led to partner with Quaneshala and I on this project, please visit www.1mdp.org to donate or to learn about other ways you can assist in helping us reach this goal. It only takes one person to make a difference. You could be that person! We look forward to hearing from you. In the meantime, spread the word about this project. Extraordinary work is taking place right now!

The Journey Begins Now

Friends, I hope you have enjoyed reading this book as much as we have enjoyed writing it. You now have all the tools to live on *The 4th Level of Financial Freedom*. We covered a lot of ground on each of the four levels. The secrets that fuel giving are no longer a mystery to you. The journey begins now.

Take the ideas you have learned, put them into practice, and share them with others. Providing other people with the hope and courage to turn their finances around will actually reinforce the financial education you have received from the pages of this book.

The people who are the closest to us sometimes have the hardest time accepting our advice. If you have family, friends, or co-workers that need financial help, but will not listen to your suggestions, buy them a copy of this book. Let them read the secrets to wealth for themselves. Later, after they finish reading the book, a one-on-one discussion with them will be beneficial. It's also a good idea to form a study group with all those who are learning and applying the valuable information found within these pages. Some awesome ideas and financial tips can come from a group that is focused on the same goal.

There are a lot of ways to change the world. Managing God's resources properly is a good place to start.

LET'S BEGIN!

Additional Information

SPEAKING ENGAGEMENTS

STRAIGHT TALK FROM THE FINANCIAL FREEDOM EXPERTS: This workshop is for anyone who would like to learn the secrets to financial freedom. It encompasses all of our counseling services (e.g. Future Stars, Mountain Climbers, Trend Setters, and Staying Together). You will learn how to make smart purchases with cash, create a realistic monthly budget, discover ways to decrease your monthly expenses, explore ways to increase your monthly income, and learn how to make decisions as a couple with a win/win attitude.

If your company, church, or organization would like us to present our Financial Freedom Workshop in your area, contact us for information on pricing and availability. We will be happy to provide you with more information.

The Financial Freedom Experts

4621 S. Cooper #131-314

Arlington, TX 76017

T: 817-677-8064

www.TheFinancialFreedomExperts.com

ONE-ON-ONE COUNSELING

FUTURE STARS: This plan is for individuals that are ready to learn the science of mastering money. We will teach you how to handle money wisely and avoid getting into debt. You will learn why it is important to start planning your future at an early age. If you want to take control of your destiny by making intelligent financial choices, this plan is for you.

MOUNTAIN CLIMBERS: This plan is for individuals that need help getting out of debt. It was designed to teach you a proven way of how to eliminate debt and build wealth. You will learn the importance of sacrificing short-term pleasure for long-term financial success. If you are stuck in a rut and need help climbing out of a mountain of debt, this plan is for you. (Most clients are able to get out of debt in less than 2 years - not including the house).

TREND SETTERS: This plan was designed for individuals that are already out of debt and want to establish a system for building wealth. If you would like to take your financial game to the next level, this plan is for you.

STAYING TOGETHER: Money is the #1 cause of marital problems. This plan was designed to help engaged and newlywed couples start their marriage making sound financial decisions. Beginning a new life with someone can be challenging without having to deal with money problems. This plan will help couples become one by managing their money as a team.

PHONE COUNSELING: We provide counseling sessions over the phone for clients that are not located in the Dallas/Ft. Worth area. You will need access to a computer, internet, phone, and a quiet meeting place where you will not be disturbed during your coaching sessions. If married, your spouse will also need to attend the session.

HOURLY RATE SESSIONS: If you have a special situation that doesn't demand a full counseling plan, then our hourly rate option may be the ideal solution for you. You will have the opportunity to ask questions pertaining to your unique situation during our talks. This session is also great for clients needing a refresher course.

Visit www.TheHeartOfATeacher.com for more information on our one-on-one counseling session.